THE FIRST
BATTLE OF
ST ALBANS

ABOUT THE AUTHOR

Andrew Boardman has written extensively on English military history. His previous books include *The Battle of Towton*, *The Medieval Soldier in the Wars of the Roses* and *Hotspur: Henry Percy, Medieval Rebel*. He also regularly lectures on the battles of the Wars of the Roses. He lives in Wakefield.

THE FIRST BATTLE OF ST ALBANS 1455

ANDREW BOARDMAN

TEMPUS

First published 2006

Tempus Publishing Limited
The Mill, Brimscombe Port,
Stroud, Gloucestershire, GL5 2QG
www.tempus-publishing.com

Typesetting and origination by Tempus Publishing Limited
Printed in Great Britain

Contents

Acknowledgements

For many years, the battle of Bosworth was traditionally regarded as the final encounter of the Wars of the Roses, purely because some commentators found it a convenient place to mark the end of one historical period and denote the beginning of another. This same reasoning also claimed that Bosworth signified the end of Richard III's 'tyrannical' rule and the creation of a new age under Henry VII, the first Tudor king. Shakespeare, among other writers, appropriated this symbolism and made it common currency in his history plays, and thus the above timelines have featured in classrooms and popular tradition ever since. However, today most historians accept that the Wars of the Roses continued well into the reign of Henry Tudor and that the final pitched battle of the wars was fought not at Bosworth in 1485 but at Stoke Field two years later. So if the battle of Stoke signified the end of the Wars of the Roses, where did York and Lancaster first cross swords?

When I was asked to write this book, I was of the opinion that the civil wars known persistently as the 'Wars of the Roses' began at Blore Heath in 1459, when Neville contingents led by the earl of Salisbury successfully beat off repeated attacks by a Lancastrian army under the command of Lord Audley. Suffice to say I have changed my opinion since. This work claims that the first battle of St Albans was not merely 'a short scuffle in a street', as Charles Oman and a number of other historians have suggested, but that it was instead a key battle of the Wars of the

Roses – that is, the series of deceptively segmented campaigns fought in England during the latter half of the fifteenth century, all sharing a common thread: the perpetuation of local and dynastic feuding. Although civil disorder and rebellions had been endemic throughout the fifteenth century, civil war had been avoided on many occasions. It is therefore not surprising that the battle of St Albans has been put into this category by critics who largely forget that the encounter remains central to our understanding of how the feuding aspect of the Wars of the Roses began. Thus, a more measured exploration of 'Saint Albans' battle, won by famous York' is long overdue.

Walking and exploring a battlefield is the only way to appreciate how a battle was fought, and I am indebted to several people who found the time to answer questions and provide expert knowledge on medieval St Albans. I would like to thank Brian Adams and Kate Warren at St Albans Museums Service for their interest in the project and for kindly reproducing the Tonman Ditch diagram. I am grateful to Chris Saunders for his professional archaeological help, and especially for enlightening me on the many aspects of medieval St Albans unknown to the casual visitor. I am indebted to Michele Seeberger for translating 'The Fastolf Relation' and to Lesley Boatwright for her rendering of Whethamstede's *Registrum*, both of whom were kindly sourced by Geoffrey Wheeler. Resolute as ever, thanks are also due to Geoff, who sacrificed the time to read through the manuscript, supplied a great many of the pictures for the book and who over the past few years has kept me well supplied with letters and information regarding the battle and related Wars of the Roses subjects. I would also like to extend my thanks to the Royal Armouries, Leeds, for kindly supplying a number of the pictures and to Phillip Abbot and Stuart Ivinson for arranging this. Kevin Bullimore at the British Library acquired some of the more obscure documents relating to the Nevilles and Percys, and the staff at Leeds and Wakefield libraries provided help with acquiring the main sources. I am also grateful to Simon Stanley for his invaluable information on the medieval bow and arrow, and, last but not least, thanks are due to all at Tempus Publishing for being so patient with me while I researched and wrote the book. There is little doubt that this work would not have been completed without the support of my family, and I am especially grateful, as always, to my wife Sheree and daughter Maisie for giving me the space and the time to write it.

Preface

The Key Field

Mowbray herald had just returned from the king, and now, after hours of waiting in Key Field to the east of St Albans, Richard of York was once again on the verge of committing treason.

Furious that his many declarations of loyalty had not been heeded, York was determined to capture his rival, the duke of Somerset, no matter what the cost. However, Henry VI's last threatening message was still ringing in Duke Richard's ears, and rather than act faithfully upon the words of a king who might be constrained by false councillors, York decided to send Mowbray herald on one last mission to the town, in an effort to avoid bloodshed.

Riding beside Duke Richard on that fateful morning in May 1455 was his brother-in-law, the 'prudent' earl of Salisbury, and pacing the embankment of St Albans' protective ditch was Salisbury's ambitious young son, Richard Neville, Earl of Warwick, later to become known as the great 'kingmaker' of Wars of the Roses legend. Both Neville earls, father and son, had swelled York's ranks with their extensive retinues, culled from those parts of northern England where violence was seen as an everyday fact of life. Now, however, with many of their border levies becoming increasingly agitated after hours of waiting, Duke Richard could see by the look on his brother-in-law's face that his famous temperance was fading fast.

By contrast, the earl of Warwick's men, clad in their distinctive red jackets emblazoned with the white ragged staff, had already edged forward towards the town, and had begun to skirmish with some of the king's men, not waiting for York to order the advance. At the forefront of Warwick's contingents, knots of border archers could be seen bracing their powerful yew bows in anticipation of battle, not to mention the fact that Sir Robert Ogle, with his 600 men of the Marches, had already crossed the town ditch, hoping to prove himself worthy of the Nevilles' trust in battle. Add to this the fact that for at least three hours a terrible sense of foreboding had lingered in York's army, due to the dreadful uncertainty of facing their rightful king in combat, and it was clear that Duke Richard had to act swiftly or suffer the disaster of disunity within his ranks.

But what if York failed in his latest effort to remove the duke of Somerset from office? What would the commons think of his decision to act forcefully against the king's wishes? How might he explain such treasonable action afterwards, if by some chance the king was injured, or even killed in the assault on the town? Alternatively, if York's bid to capture Somerset succeeded, how could he permanently remove his rival from the king's inner circle once his Neville supporters had disbanded their contingents? In short, what crucial decision might Duke Richard have to take in order to release Somerset's seditious hold over the king?

There was still enough time for York to step back from the abyss, but the argument as to who should rule England if King Henry succumbed to another bout of mental illness was unmistakably one-sided. The only course of action was for York to extract Somerset by force, and thereby cut a new cloth of state with cold Milanese steel. With his thirteen-year-old son, Edward, Earl of March, watching his every move, it would be too much for York's pride to shrink from a fight. But as Mowbray herald yet again spurred his horse towards the town, carrying York's protestations of innocence, the duke knew that his next move would have to be decisive.

It was an age-old feud that would be responsible for opening hostilities at St Albans, but for both sides the first blow struck would inflict a much deeper wound that would prove terminal. What historians would later call the 'Wars of the Roses' were about to be instigated, but no one that day could ever have anticipated the long-term effects of the first battle of St Albans, nor prophesy how the bloodletting there would eventually sign the death warrants of a substantial portion of England's medieval nobility.

I

York and Somerset

Richard Plantagenet, third Duke of York, like most medieval nobles, wanted to be liked by his contemporaries, yet this seemingly innocent ambition – to appear the perfect champion of law and order and the model protector of England – was never fully realised in his lifetime.

Despite several attempts at political mediation, not to mention various bouts of what might have been dubbed treasonable activity, York was destined to fail miserably time and time again in his efforts to remove political rivals from office, chiefly because his noble and somewhat impetuous character always got in the way of sound political judgement. Chivalric pride was a quality that most fifteenth-century nobles understood, and would readily die for if the cause benefited themselves or their family, and therefore it was no surprise that York's self-righteous and reckless ambition would eventually lead to a copybook chivalrous death at the hands of those who had been injured by his rise to power. We may question York's rash paladin nature, his ambition and his pride, but was this noble recklessness the chief cause of his downfall, as some historians suggest? In short, was the duke of York completely loyal to the crown during his lifetime, even after the watershed battle of St Albans, or was he, in fact, an opportunist whose aim was to usurp the throne in place of Henry VI, who by contemporary standards was clearly unfit to rule England?

A considerable body of written evidence survives concerning the duke of York's vast inheritance, his official correspondence and his military appointments. However, as with so many historical figures, no accurate character assessment of York is possible, other than to say that, on face value, his sense of nobility far outweighed his recklessness. Many times, in his letters and petitions to the king, we are reminded of Richard's apparent loyalty and determination 'as the King's true liegeman and serv-ant... to advise his Royal Majesty of certain articles concerning the weal and safeguard, as well of his most royal person, as the tranquillity and conservation of all this his realm'.[1] York also wished to remove the king's enemies, including Edmund Beaufort, Duke of Somerset and his support-ers, all of whom, in his own words, 'laboureth continually about the King's highness for my undoing'[2] – clearly an opinion that can be taken both ways. Therefore, in the absence of an impartial character witness, there is much of Richard of York's persona that must remain hidden from view.

It is also a matter of great frustration that no description or faith-ful image survives of medieval personalities other than a number of sketches in manuscripts and several statues, which in most instances contain misinformation and portray an invented image. In York's case, the most famous of these is the stained-glass window at Trinity College, Cambridge, which shows him wearing full armour, while another similar depiction in Cirencester parish church reveals the face of a slightly frail character, clearly not in keeping with the attitude of one of the most powerful men in England. However, in written evidence York's immedi-ate family provide the best clue to the duke's outward appearance. It was evidently well known to contemporaries that he resembled his youngest son, also named Richard (later Richard III), who, during the defama-tory campaign aimed at bastardising his brother Edward IV in 1483, was noted by the well-informed foreign observer Dominic Mancini as 'altogether resembling his father'.[3]

Richard 'Plantagenet' was born on 21 September 1411 into an infamous family which inherited its royal blood from the patriarch of all late medieval kings, Edward III, through his two sons, Edmund, Duke of York and Lionel, Duke of Clarence. Richard was an only son and his renowned claim to greatness and dynastic claim to the English throne can be explained on two counts. His mother, Anne Mortimer, was the sister of Edmund, Earl of March, whose family had been the focus of many political intrigues and threats against the crown in the past. Most conspicuously, this antagonism was aimed at the Lancastrian claimant to the throne, Henry Bolingbroke, whose usurpation of 1399 later formed part of Yorkist propaganda in the Wars of the Roses. On the paternal side of York's family, his father, Richard, Earl of Cambridge, was executed for high treason in what later became known as the Southampton Plot against Henry V in 1415. This terrible association was one that the young Richard of York had to bear throughout his life and, indeed, it may have been a stigma that weighed heavily on his character and fortunes in adulthood. However, apart from the obvious antipathy felt to any such treasonable behaviour against the crown, York was never tainted with his father's crime. Also, Richard's uncle, Edward, Duke of York, had died loyal to the Lancastrian cause at the battle of Agincourt in 1415, and thus York's family, at least on the ascendant branch, had redeemed itself in blood.

Soon after Henry V's glowing victories in France, the young Richard was placed, like most noble offspring, with trusted mentors, to learn the 'gentle' arts of nobility and chivalry. In Richard's case this was with Sir Robert Waterton, an old Yorkshire knight and veteran of the French Wars. No better-skilled campaigner could have been chosen for York, but in 1423 it was decided that the young duke should be transferred to the earl of Westmoreland's care for nine years, and doubtless it was here that he learned much about the Neville family and their Beaufort connections from Joan, Westmoreland's second wife.

On the death of the earl of March in 1425, great changes began to shape Richard's life, and soon the vast Mortimer inheritance of his uncle became the main focus of his attention. In May 1426 York was knighted, along with the new 'infant' king Henry VI, at the Leicester parliament, and in November 1429 he was summoned to attend Henry's lavish coronation at Westminster Abbey. It was not long after this that York began to take up his rightful position at court, and as duke of York he was present at Henry's fateful crowning as king of France in Paris – a notable achievement for any English monarch, but a legacy left by the new king's warrior father that his saintly son could never hope to equal.

A queen for the young King Henry had not yet been found, but a bride for Duke Richard had been determined for him when he was only thirteen. In 1426 he had married into the respected and powerful northern family with whom he had spent much of his youth. The Nevilles were equally pleased with their daughter Cecily's marriage into the house of York and, like many other large and ambitious medieval dynasties before them, they doubtless saw Duke Richard's claim to fame and fortune as a means to advance their own position in northern England.

By 1445, the duke of York had become acquainted with his vast lordship and had as a result secured the services of many notable knights and retainers, as befitted his position, including Ralph Lord Cromwell, Thomas Lord Scales, Sir John Falstolf, Sir Andrew Ogard, Sir William ap Thomas and Sir William Oldhall, the latter figuring in the important political events which followed his master's enforced exile in Ireland in 1450. Also prominent among Richard's many connections at this time were members of the powerful Bourchier family, Viscount Bourchier being recorded as York's chief councillor in 1448; and, more significantly with regard to the battle of St Albans, Richard became related to Thomas Bourchier, who became chancellor and archbishop of Canterbury in 1454. The Bourchiers were the powerful half-brothers of Richard's aunt, the countess of March, and York's only sister Isabel was married to Henry Bourchier, all alliances which would prove of crucial importance to the duke later on in his career. Duke Richard's links to these and several other important baronial houses made him an extremely powerful man in his own right, but by the time he finally gained his Mortimer inheritance, provided he honoured the outstanding obligations of his two dead uncles, he was able to boast vast landholdings in almost every English county. He also owned properties in the Marches of Wales and in Ireland, while on his maternal grandmother's side he benefited from being known as the earl of March and Ulster and the lord of Wigmore, Clare, Trim and Connaught, the latter titles providing him with a foothold in Ireland and, by coincidence, a safe haven where he might take refuge in times of trouble or personal crisis.

Like most men of his age, York had already seen military service in France, but it was not until 1436 that he formally agreed by indenture to serve as the king's lieutenant-general in Normandy, an appointment that was to lead to several dismissals and recalls, all resulting in a vast personal debt that was never repaid in full by the crown. Richard Beauchamp, Earl of Warwick was appointed to succeed York as lieutenant in 1437, but when he died two years later the chief command of English armies in France devolved to John Beaufort, then earl of Somerset. As a nephew of the extremely powerful and politically minded Cardinal Beaufort, the earl of Somerset could, like York, trace his royal blood back to Edward III, through John of Gaunt and his second wife, Catherine Swynford. However, Somerset's line of descent had been barred and so was no threat to York at this time, although it was a claim that, if legitimised, could provide an heir to the throne should Henry VI remain childless.

Somerset was an extremely inept general, but when York's bid to provoke Charles VII into fighting a pitched battle failed, the king's council decided that he should take York's place – a decision that was to result in York's distrust of the entire Beaufort family and, most notably, was to lead to his dread of a possible competitor for the succession. Advanced by his uncle, the extremely wealthy cardinal, and given a dukedom to enhance his authority, Somerset crossed the English Channel in August 1443 and proceeded to pillage La Guerche, a town belonging to the friendly duke of Brittany. Incurring not only the anger of York but also the great displeasure of the English government, Somerset's appointment proved to be a complete disaster. However, given the fact that the war was slowly turning in favour of the French, who still refused to fight pitched battles against the English, Somerset was not the first to suffer a severe reprimand from those who had appointed him. Recalled to England, the earl died the following year, leaving the new duke, Edmund Beaufort, as direct competition to York's supremacy.

York continued to command in France, despite lack of financial help, but his ambitions to emulate the English successes of Crécy and Agincourt were ingloriously dashed on several occasions. Instead, the duke was given more commercial and civil duties, and in 1445 he was appointed to accompany Margaret of Anjou, his future enemy, to the French coast before she embarked for England to marry Henry VI. However, the political wheel of fortune was about to turn full circle against Duke Richard when he, like Somerset before him, was ordered to return home on the pretext that his presence was required at the coming parliament. York's term of office in France had in fact expired, but Richard obviously hoped to be recalled at some later date as, in theory at least, he was the obvious choice for lieutenant, now that the Beauforts were discredited.

Evidently Duke Richard had no idea what the court party was planning against him at this time or he would have acted immediately, but the essential mechanism that brought about York's recall and later 'banishment' was clearly the design of a group of unscrupulous nobles who sought to control the king and, in so doing, enhance their own positions at court. However, given the names of the ringleaders in this conspiracy, it is also apparent that broader politics, and a complex web of existing retainers and 'well-willers', added fuel to the political fire.

It is no accident that the politics which brought York into direct opposition with Edmund, the new duke of Somerset, were initially manufactured by the ambitions of lesser courtiers hoping to carve out a career at the expense of a malleable and ineffective king. However, King Henry must also bear a major portion of the blame, and to appreciate this further it is essential, as far as possible, to understand the king's complex character. In his fulsome assessment of Henry's saintly nature, John Blacman, the king's confessor, makes plain the absurdity of his sovereign's 'monkish' kingship:

> He was like a second Job, a man simple and upright, altogether fearing the Lord God, and departing from evil. He was a simple man, without any crook of craft or untruth, as is plain to all. With none did he deal craftily, nor ever would say an untrue word to any, but framed his speech always to speak the truth... The lord king complained to me once in his room at Eltham, when I was alone with him and working with him over his holy books, and hearing his serious admonitions and devout observations, one of the most powerful of the English dukes knocked on the door. The king said: 'See how they disturb me!'[4]

This depiction of Henry's devout and other-worldly nature is contrary to what other commentators thought of him, and there is no contemporary evidence to suggest the king was uniquely addicted to prayer or private meditation. Indeed, he could be both spiteful and vindictive, and his apparent failure to appreciate what was going on in the real world was, in fact, one of the main causes of the Wars of the Roses. All his life, apart from faint glimpses of adroit kingship, others controlled him to the extent that one biased chronicler later described him as 'of small intelligence'.[5] However, it is clear that much of this character assassination was later anti-Lancastrian propaganda, and that during his youth there was no reason to suppose that Henry might not turn out to be a replica of his formidable father. Among the chroniclers who bemoaned the passing of Henry V was John Hardyng, and at about the time of the first battle of St Albans he wrote a eulogy in praise of the victor of Agincourt which compares the rule of both father and son:

> O good lord God, why did you let so soon to pass
> This noble prince [Henry V], that in all Christianity
> Had then no peer in any land, no more nor less;
> So excellent was his happy truth
> In flourishing age of all freshness of youth
> That might have let him live to greater age
> Till he had wholly gained his heritage.
>
> The peace at home and law so well maintained
> Were root and head of all his great conquest,
> Which exiled is away and foully now distained
> In such degree that north and south and west
> And east also enjoys now little rest,
> But by day and night in every shire throughout
> With sallets bright and jacks make fearful rout.[6]

Such was the exhortation levelled at Henry VI in adulthood, at a time when many men must have known how lawless some parts of the kingdom had become. Clearly, Hardyng's scathing words did not express his opinion alone, and this, aside from the obvious propaganda, points to a weakness in both the king and his government. However, this was not the only reason for the steady decline mentioned above.

From as early as 1 September 1422, the government of England had been carried on in the name of Henry VI by a select council of peers, the king then being a minor and not yet old enough to rule the kingdom alone. It was common medieval practice for the king's uncles to take precedence during a minority, but Humphrey, Duke of Gloucester, Henry V's younger brother, had reluctantly become part of a ruling council in which the Beauforts were his most quarrelsome enemies. With the crown virtually out of commission for a time, one would have expected that these two factions would have come to blows on more than one occasion, but this was not the case and business was carried on as usual in the name of the king. However, the political history of the next ten years disclosed an underlying conflict, established in 1437, which brought about factionalism and division when Henry emerged from his minority a less 'forceful' monarch than medieval England deserved. Thus it was only a matter of time before the most dominant court faction took control of the 'malleable' king, and as the war with France turned unmistakeably sour this inner circle became headed essentially by William de la Pole, later duke of Suffolk, and a group of clergy guided by bishops Ayscough of Salisbury and Moleyns of Chichester.

The public denunciation of these three men leaves no doubt that they were chiefly responsible for the disasters that followed, both at home and abroad. After Gloucester's mysterious death in 1447, Suffolk, in particular, succeeded in making King Henry his puppet while at the same time removing many of the enemies who stood in his way. This process of control and indoctrination was, of course, a gradual development, but in July 1446 the duke of York had been involved in a violent quarrel with Adam Moleyns, then Henry's Keeper of the Privy Seal, whom he accused of bribing his troops so that they would charge him with embezzlement. The result had been a serious breach with the court party who, in the course of their machinations, caused York's recall to England and the appointment of Edmund Beaufort, Duke of Somerset to the lieutenancy of France. York's 'punishment' was clearly galling, and even more so when he was appointed lieutenant of Ireland for the unusual term of ten years. Evidently, Suffolk and the court party wanted York out of the way for purely personal reasons, and by using King Henry's pliability and power to impose their will they largely succeeded in achieving their aim.

Soon, from his exile in Ireland, York had the dubious satisfaction of hearing that yet another Beaufort was leading English armies to disaster in France. It is significant that at the end of York's term of office in Normandy and his removal to Ireland in 1447 Henry's dwindling exchequer owed him £38,666, an enormous sum of money at the time, part of which the duke renounced and the remainder of which he aimed to recover at a later date. The resulting French losses, caused by the well-financed Somerset, therefore injured York on two counts, at a time when he was both physically and politically constrained in exile. By the tone of his later letters, denouncing Somerset's conduct in France, it was a personal humiliation that cut him to the core.

But was there yet another reason why York was being excluded from the king's council? Abbot Whethamstede, the chronicler who recorded the first and second battles of St Albans, had no doubt that York's dynastic claim to the throne was the true source for his arrogant and uncontrolled quest for power in the 1450s. Richard, as Henry's heir apparent, had every reason to fear the ambitions of Somerset, especially when his rival came to entrench himself deep within the king's inner council. In essence, the fear that Somerset might be officially recognised as the Lancastrian heir if ever Henry VI should die childless was probably the main reason for Whethamstede's scathing remarks about York's ambitious nature. Another motive was that the abbot probably harboured intense feelings against the duke because of his subsequent attack on and pillage of St Albans in 1455.

However, it was clear that York could ill afford to overlook the Beaufort claims to the throne, and doubtless this was the main reason for his feud with Somerset. As for the duke of Suffolk, the chief instigator of all York's troubles, he did not live long enough to see his political intrigues come to fruition. In January 1450, the commons, awakening to the frightening losses in France as well as the tides of discontent and lawlessness at home, conveniently placed the blame for the current misfortunes on Suffolk's ambitious head. It was clear that the court party needed a scapegoat, and it was undoubtedly to Somerset's benefit that someone else was available to take the blame. The exclusion of Suffolk was a travesty, brought about by an ineffective king and a series of events that were undoubtedly arranged by other ambitious guiding hands. When the commons tried to impeach Suffolk, the king's 'merciful' intervention only helped to delay the inevitable. In the event, a term of banishment was placed on the duke and, consequently, when his boat pulled away from the Kentish coast there was already a plot to kill him:

> ...and one of the lewdest of the ship bade him lay down his head [so] that he might be fairly dealt with and die on a sword; and [he] took a rusty sword and smote of his head with half a dozen strokes, and [he] took away his gown of russet and his doublet of velvet mailed, and laid his body on the sands of Dover; and some say his head was set on a pole by it.[7]

Banishment for five years was clearly a sentence that a man like Suffolk could have easily survived but, as fate would have it, the duke was considered a worthy scapegoat for all England's troubles. The kind of unrest that was virulent in the kingdom, and the general disorder that was rife, especially in Kent, only added to the mounting problems that King Henry and his corrupt government had to deal with. Indeed, their troubles went from bad to worse, and it is clear that the insurrection and rebellion led by Jack Cade in May-July 1450 was symptomatic of the growing dissatisfaction with many of the king's chief ministers. Once more, the cry of 'Mortimer' was used to signal popular rebellion in English shires, and by the time hundreds of Kentish insurgents reached the gates of London, news of Cade's murderous rampage had spread far and wide. The volatile situation could only have added to York's fears, especially when news reached him in Ireland that his name was being used in the rebel's manifesto as the man most likely to bring about reform. The Kentish rebels were adamant that the king should

> ...take about his noble person his true blood of his royal realm, that is to say, the high and mighty prince, the duke of York, exiled from our sovereign lord's person by the noising of the false traitor the duke of Suffolk and his affinity.[8]

It was a situation that York, and his enemy Somerset, could not fail to ignore, even though the rebellion was soon put down and its ringleaders executed for high treason. With characteristic blindness, the final act of the king's council was to recall Somerset from France and duly appoint him constable of England, in order to deal with any further disturbances at home. Despite failing dismally in Normandy, he was given every opportunity and assistance to establish law and order in the country, including the power to co-ordinate resistance against the problematic return of Duke Richard, who, due to Cade's 'slanderous' manifesto, had already taken alarm and landed in north Wales.

York's return can only have caused a great deal of panic among the court party, although it is clear that, according to a letter sent by him prior to his arrival in England, he was not aiming to displace anyone in the king's council. Waiting jealously in Ireland for a message to recall him to England can hardly have soothed the feelings of injustice and frustration that York must have suffered at this time. Somerset and his friends evidently wanted York permanently exiled, and in fact must have feared for their own lives when he cleverly managed to avoid several ambushes on his way to London. After these attempts on his life, York clearly had no choice but to protect himself. Since it is said that he raised an army of some 4,000 men, it was no surprise that the animosity between York and Somerset soon entered a new and dangerous phase.

Forcing his way into the king's apartments may have been one way for York to put his point across to Henry, but the king's 'kindly' demeanour dampened Duke Richard's hot-headedness and ultimately postponed all the inevitable questions that still surrounded the government. A rash petition in parliament for the recognition of Duke Richard as Henry's heir, made by the member for Bristol, Thomas Young, was yet another personal presumption that York could have done without at this time. However, even as Young was conducted to the Tower for his impulsive behaviour, it was apparent to all present, including York's enemies, that others might raise the same dynastic question if King Henry's marriage remained unfruitful.

On the face of it, Duke Richard's first attempt to bring about reform had failed, and Somerset retained his position as Henry's chief councillor. However, York's rash behaviour was a taste of things to come; in the autumn of 1450 he took a different course of action and used the petition he had previously brought before Henry to try and enlist the help of parliament. In the end, York failed to gain support from his Neville in-laws, but he managed to solicit the help of the duke of Norfolk and the earl of Devon, who, by coincidence, were both pursuing personal feuds of their own design. Of course, York could count on his many tenants and followers for additional support in his bid to overthrow the government, but such personal adherents were useless in matters of state – what York needed was political muscle in the right quarter at the right time and, if necessary, bows and bills on hand if his petitions failed to have the desired effect. It is ironic that while York was trying to pursue a policy of peace in order to remove his enemy Somerset, other lesser ministers were yet again exploiting his name and his 'famous' dynastic claim by promoting political unease.

As early as March 1450, William Oldhall, York's chamberlain, had been associated with cries to remove Henry VI and have his master acclaimed king. He spread the rumour that Henry, by the advice of Suffolk, had sold the realm of England to the king of France, a claim that was obviously ludicrous in the extreme, but nonetheless a lie of sufficient substance to make any of York's petitions aimed at political reform appear utterly worthless. In fact, the appointment of the duke of Somerset to the captaincy of Calais in 1451 gives credence to the theory that York's appeals and constant petitioning were becoming tiresome to all but a minority. Somerset's appointment to command the largest military establishment at the king's disposal also indicated that, even after his failure in France, Henry still had every confidence in his abilities.

Finding himself more politically isolated than ever, the duke of York now sought to remove Somerset by force. Obviously, York was in a very dangerous position, but although he has been noted historically chiefly for his recklessness, he was on this occasion very prudent in his preparations. He had previously sought support in the Welsh Marches in order to protect himself from his enemies, and now that support was called upon yet again, in the form of an armed demonstration. However, York was careful not to alienate himself from King Henry, and on 9 January 1452 he signed and sealed a declaration protesting his loyalty. On 3 February, from his castle at Ludlow, he also wrote to the town of Shrewsbury stressing the danger to the country now that Somerset was in command of the Calais garrison:

> Right worshipful friends, I recommend me unto you; and I suppose it is well known unto you, as well by experience as by common language said and reported throughout all Christendom, what laud, what worship, honour, and manhood, was ascribed of all nations unto the people of this realm whilst the kingdom's sovereign lord stood possessed of his lordship in the realm of France and duchy of Normandy; and what derogation, loss of merchandize, lesion of honour, and villainy, is said and reported generally unto the English nation for the loss of the same; namely unto the Duke of Somerset, when he had the commandance and charge thereof...Wherefore, worshipful friends, to the intent that every man shall know my purpose and desire for to declare me such as I am, I signify unto you that, with the help and supportation of Almighty God, and of Our Lady, and of all the Company of Heaven, I, after long sufferance and delays, [though it is] not my will or intent to displease my sovereign lord, seeing that the said duke ever prevaileth and ruleth about the king's person, and that by this means the land is likely to be destroyed, I am fully concluded to proceed in all haste against him with the help of my kinsmen and friends...[9]

York further warned that, 'the said Duke of Somerset... laboureth continually about the king's highness for my undoing',[10] and urged several other English towns to help him restore good governance to the realm – a clear sign that he not only feared for his own safety, but also for the safety of England.

Despite the winter season, York was successful in raising a large force and, with the help of the earl of Devon and his henchman Lord Cobham, his army was soon on the march, taking a route towards London that allowed him to muster further support in the south Midlands and along the Severn valley. On 22 and 26 February, he was met by a delegation of lords sent by the king, wishing to know his intentions. York stated that his aim was not to harm the king's person, but he explained that certain 'traitors' who had brought about the ruin of the country would answer for their crimes. When news of his claims reached King Henry and his ministers, orders were dispatched for London to close its gates, forcing the duke's army to divert across Kingston Bridge into Kent, where, at least in theory, the 'Yorkists', as we now must call them, hoped to gather more support.

Meanwhile, the royal army, including retinues supplied by the earls of Salisbury and Warwick and the duke of Buckingham, had marched south from Northampton. In fact, by the time York encamped his army at Dartford in Kent, Henry's forces had been augmented and were also commanded by a number of York's friends and relatives, including the duke of Norfolk, who had previously supported his cause. With the prospect of little or no Kentish support forthcoming, York suddenly found himself trapped between an angle of the river Thames and the royal host with banners displayed for war. Fate had dealt another cruel hand to York. With neither hope of reinforcement nor the prospect of retreat open to him, he had no option but to fortify his position near Crayford, at a place called Sandhill, where apparently 3,000 gunners fronted his army. The *London Chronicle* gives an account of what followed:

And the Duke of York pitched his field about Dartford with great ordnance. And whilst the king lay still at St Mary Overey's, bishops rode between the king and the Duke of York to set them at rest and peace. But the Duke of York said he would have the Duke of Somerset, or else he would die therefore. And on Wednesday next following [1 March] the king with his host rode to Blackheath, and forth over Shooters Hill to Welling, and there lodged that day and the morrow. And on Thursday at afternoon there was made an appointment between the king and the Duke of York by the mean of his lords. And on the morrow, that was Friday, the king assembled his host on the Blackheath afore noon; and there abode the coming of the Duke of York.[11]

Both sides were now in a position to fight; however, it is questionable whether either York or the royalists desired to pursue military action. The next few hours were to have a critical impact on the way York and his Neville in-laws would conduct themselves at the first battle of St Albans, but – contrary to the events of 1455, where battle was joined after protracted discussions – it was the earls of Salisbury and Warwick, along with Thomas Bourchier, later archbishop of Canterbury, who were charged with opening negotiations, to avert the shedding of English blood.

York at first stood by his original purpose of accusing Somerset of high treason, and stated that only if his rival was immediately detained and put on trial would he disband his army. The Nevilles ostensibly agreed with these aims, and when the king was advised of York's stance he apparently gave his verbal assent to a formal inquiry. However, when the Yorkist army stood down, on trust that Somerset would be confined and questioned, Duke Richard found to his dismay that he had been tricked, in the worst possible way. In fact, when he and the Nevilles arrived at the king's tent, with a small escort, Somerset was found to be at liberty and in his accustomed seat beside the king. It was evident that with or without the Nevilles' collusion York had walked straight into a trap, and that soon he would be forced to answer charges of treason. He was first confined to his house in London and later forced to swear a solemn oath of loyalty to King Henry at St Paul's – it was a victory that Somerset no doubt relished to the full, and one that York would remember in 1455.

York's quarrel with his rival had yet again backfired, and he returned to Ludlow a bitter man. He had showed his hand openly, first by petition and finally by force of arms, but it was now the turn of the court party to strike back, which they did by punishing several of Duke Richard's adherents and 'co-conspirators', including the earl of Devon and Lord Cobham, who were both imprisoned awaiting trial. Sir William Oldhall was also indicted for his traitorous behaviour, and later he was attainted for spreading unrest in the shires. Thus, in the summer of 1453 Richard of York was yet again forced into exile – this time on his own estates, while abroad, against all the odds, the English army in France had seized

Bordeaux and was expected to recover it, led by the renowned captain John Talbot, Earl of Shrewsbury.

At home, to add insult to injury, York's lieutenancy of Ireland was stripped from him and given over to the earl of Wiltshire, a courtier who, as we will later see, was conspicuous for his aptitude for survival on the battlefield. Meanwhile, York had no other option but to bide his time and wait for Somerset's position to become more vulnerable. In July 1453 this opening seemed highly unlikely, but when the redoubtable Talbot was killed and his army routed, at the battle of Castillion, there was a complete reversal of fortunes. When the king received this terrible news at his hunting lodge at Clarendon he went suddenly mad from the shock, while Somerset was in attendance. This association, along with the total loss of Aquitaine, caused a tide of popular anger against the duke that he would never be able to shake off, although it cannot be proven that he had anything directly to do with either event.

However, apart from the problems in France, a king who was mentally and physically inert was something that could neither be hidden nor tolerated. Something had to be done, and the protracted debate as to whether Henry could ever stay sane for a reasonable period of time came to a head when the king's council were put in the unenviable position of appointing a regent. Months passed before anything constructive was done, and by this time the dynastic question was further complicated by an unexpected new arrival: on 13 October 1453 the queen gave birth to a son, an event that effectively cancelled out any thoughts of succession by either York or Somerset. It was clear that the political wheel of fortune was once again turning, and its workings yet again placed Duke Richard in a perfect position at its central axis, despite everything. Due to Henry's tragic infirmity (probably catatonic schizophrenia), York found himself firstly appointed back onto the king's council and, secondly, nominated as Protector. Even though the problem of the succession had been solved by natural means – namely the birth of Edward, Prince of Wales – York's newfound title afforded him wide-ranging powers, and he immediately used them to the full by attacking his enemy Somerset from a position of strength. The unfortunate duke, weakened by the recent fateful events, was immediately stripped of his captaincy of Calais, charged with treason and confined to the Tower awaiting trial. The way was now open for York to appoint his own administration, and it was no accident that personal feuding in Wales and the north and south-west of England coloured his thinking.

In the 1450s, it is certain that none of the aristocracy or their adherents would have been known as either a 'Yorkist' or a 'Lancastrian' supporter, but certain divisions had already been formed, due to Duke Richard's political and military demonstrations. Therefore it is hardly surprising that after the king became incapacitated York gave prominence to his supporters when it came to filling the council chamber. In April 1454, he managed to secure the nomination of his own brother-in-law, the fifty-four-year-old earl of Salisbury, as chancellor of England. Salisbury, whose sons were engaged in a violent Yorkshire feud with the duke of Exeter and the Percy family, was eager to lend the new Protector help, for reasons of his own, and in an effort to solve more local issues the Nevilles received somewhat biased support from the government. Also prominent in Duke Richard's council at this time were members of the Bourchier family, while, in contrast, neither the duke of Exeter nor the earl of Northumberland played any great part in York's administration. From now on the question of loyalty to an anointed king would never have the same meaning; factionalism was fast becoming a much more dangerous weapon to employ if one wished to survive.

But what did the duke of Somerset think of York's recent victory and protectorate? Had Edmund Beaufort consciously manipulated Henry VI to the point of no return – in fact, pushed him to the very brink of insanity? Apart from his failure in France (where others had failed before him), what other crimes had Somerset committed against the kingdom? He had obviously not displeased King Henry and, contrary to what the duke of York claimed in his many petitions, he had not committed treason in the traditional sense of the word. His 'constant labouring' about the king's person may have given many courtiers cause for concern, but clearly the king thought Somerset, and others like him, worthy councillors, or he would have immediately taken steps to remove them. As for Henry's mental state before his breakdown in 1453, there is every reason to believe that he ruled adequately, apart from several lapses in judgement, and that he had single-handedly defused some very difficult situations. Evidently the king had his faults, one of which was his misplaced trust in others, but prior to his madness he had shown signs of kingship that were certainly not the musings of an imbecile incapable of personal rule. After all, during his minority Henry had been tutored by the best military and scholastic minds in the land, and his only failing seems to have been that he found it difficult, if not impossible, to equal the perfect portrayal of medieval kingship that his father had expounded so effectively on the battlefields of France.

On the face of it, Somerset seems to have been guilty of gross mis-management, but how much of this image was a direct result of York's political pressure and personal ambition, not to mention his much-promoted dynastic aspirations prior to the birth of the Prince of Wales? As with all personal historical relationships, the line is hard to draw with any certainty. Richard was, above all, an honourable man, but he was also a fifteenth-century nobleman who, in order to survive, had to secure his position on a daily basis. This was also true of his contemporaries, including Somerset and all those other English nobles who sought to enhance their power and position, sometimes at the expense of others. The Nevilles and Percys fit this description so perfectly that, in order to further analyse what occurred in the streets of St Albans on 22 May 1455, it is essential that a great northern feud is examined, the effects of which one chronicler blamed for the 'beginning of the greatest sorrows in England'.[12]

2

The Beginning of
Sorrows

Any study of the first battle of St Albans must also take into account the effects of the local feuding that had become widespread in some parts of England during the early 1450s. Indeed, it can be said that the first battle of St Albans was primarily a continuation of hostilities between the Neville and Percy families, and that the dukes of York and Somerset were drawn into a conflict initiated by others. This hypothesis certainly holds true with regard to the way the battle began, but it can also be argued that other nobles and their adherents paved the way for factionalism to occur on a much more dangerous scale. In particular, two lords who were chiefly responsible for the Yorkshire risings of 1453 – Henry Holand, Duke of Exeter, and the violent and extremely unpredictable Thomas Percy, Lord Egremont – fuelled those fires of discontent that created division immediately prior to the battle. It was this lesser faction, primarily influenced by the Percys, which brought about the alliance of Neville and York and proved so dangerous to the duke of Somerset in 1455.

It will be noted that neither the duke of Exeter nor Lord Egremont fought at the first battle of St Albans, but it was chiefly their actions in the north (and the way the Nevilles were overprotected by York in his official capacity as Protector) that caused a 'Yorkist' split, following the release of Somerset from the Tower in March 1455. However, it was certainly not the case that the Nevilles automatically sided with their cousin York against Somerset, or that the house of Percy supported the king purely out of loyalty or from hatred of the Nevilles. Rather, it was a series of complex connections and events that brought about the 'Yorkist' alliance of 1455 and, in time, the formation of the 'Lancastrian' party which opposed it in the civil wars of 1459.

Rekindled immediately after the war with Scotland in 1448, the relationship between Neville and Percy slowly deteriorated when the balance of power was influenced, not for the first time in history, by those in command of the northern Marches. However, the real danger came from an unexpected quarter, and this new breed of vengeance had its primary origins in the younger members of both the Neville and the Percy families. Contrary to popular opinion, the resulting northern blood feud only erupted after 1453, chiefly as a result of the Nevilles, who managed to outstrip the Percys' wealth, power and favour in Yorkshire to such an extent that the latter had to resort to violence in order to survive. Before this date, local rivalry between the families had existed for several generations, but 'open' violence had not been actively pursued by them, chiefly due to the demise of Percy autonomy during the reign of Henry IV. Crucially, it was at St Albans in 1455, when the Percys and their adherents fell foul of a supreme bout of Neville bitterness, that matters were brought to a head. Indeed, the resulting vendetta proved to be so intense that the family quarrel was not fully settled until the earl of Warwick was killed at the battle of Barnet in 1471.

Prior to 1450, both families had been forced into co-operating against Scottish raiding, and on numerous occasions local rivalries had been put aside in favour of joint action against the common foe. Warfare of this kind was intermittent and primarily seasonal, but full-scale battles had been fought throughout the medieval period, with significant loss of life, and thus members of the northern aristocracy had been periodically appointed Wardens of the Marches to combat this threat to the border. Ever since the time of 'Hotspur' and his father Henry Percy, first Earl of Northumberland, peace treaties with the Scots had rarely been taken seriously, but the warden's office, permanently instigated in the reign of Richard II, was coveted as a means to establish power not only in the north, but also in the king's council. It was crucial that the reigning monarch could count on his northern lords and their retainers to support the existing infrastructure of border recruitment whenever Scotland threatened to invade England. However, the disgrace of the Percys in 1403 and 1405, along with the disaster of Northumberland's death at the battle of Bramham Moor in 1408, had crippled Percy fortunes significantly. In short, it was some years before Hotspur's son could achieve anything like his grandfather's supremacy in the north, and it was no accident that by the time the second earl of Northumberland recovered his title in 1416 the Nevilles had equalled, if not surpassed, the Percy achievement.

However, when Ralph Neville, Earl of Westmoreland, died in 1425, the contest for territory had become not only a Neville and Percy issue, but also an internal power struggle which the earl of Salisbury set about pursuing within his own family. In fact, while the Nevilles were at odds with each other from within, Northumberland was also busy making enemies elsewhere in Yorkshire. For example, Archbishop Kemp was determined to extend his secular rights into Percy territory, and in 1441 and 1447 fighting broke out between the retainers of both sides, during which lives were lost. The irony of these particular bouts of violence was that during the 1440s it was not only the Nevilles and Percys who pursued one another in Yorkshire, but also other nobles wishing to capitalise on their instability.

All this changed in 1453, when the Percys, still struggling to rehabilitate themselves after the attainder and disgrace of the first earl, were irreverently pushed aside by a sudden bout of Neville aggrandisement. A rapid deterioration in relationships, caused by a disparity in wealth, plus the fact that the Nevilles had far stronger connections, had an enormous effect on Percy fortunes, and in the end it forced the younger members of Northumberland's family over the edge. How had the earl of Salisbury managed to create all this enmity in such a short space of time? Evidently, it had been the result of extending his northern domains at the expense of others and procuring a number of lucrative marriages and positions for his relatives, offspring and retainers. In short, the Nevilles had succeeded where the Percys had failed. They had entered the medieval property and marriage market in a big way, and once established they began to extend their hold over their rivals with unforgiving precision.

George Neville, for example, had been married to a northern heiress and had succeeded to the barony of Latimer, which boasted extensive lands in Richmondshire and Cumberland. However, he was certified as insane in the 1440s, and the earl of Salisbury succeeded in acquiring his brother's estates to augment his own in 1451. This in turn led to his re-appointment as Warden of the West March, which he received for a term of twenty years. Another brother, William Lord Fauconberg, a notable veteran of the French wars, had also married an heiress who held estates in Cleveland, and this became another important area of Neville influence in the north-east of England. However, the most important position of power had been attained by another of Salisbury's four brothers. Robert Neville was installed as bishop of Durham in 1438, and in his official capacity he was able to put the resources of his palatinate at Salisbury's disposal whenever the need arose. Add to this the fact that Edward Neville, Lord Abergavenny, through his marriage into the Beauchamp family, had also secured his family a tenuous foothold in Wales, and it only remained for Salisbury to manufacture for his son Richard the grand prize of the Warwick inheritance to make the Neville achievement complete. By 1449, when Richard Neville gained this earldom, Salisbury's family owned vast tracts of land between the Pennines and the east coast that extended fifty miles northwards, from Wensleydale to the Tyne. No wonder the Percys stood in awe of their hegemony.

As might be expected, along with all these new lucrative titles and estates came an extensive network of dependants and retainers, all willing to give faithful service to a good lord who could maintain them in the law courts and, if need be, on the battlefield. With such territorial advantage and willing manpower at his fingertips, it was evidently Salisbury's intention to make the wardenship of the West March hereditary, and thereby control the Scottish border. It was a situation that was bound to cause conflict, and in answer to this over-mighty behaviour the younger Percys lashed out in a spate of organised guerrilla warfare that took the Nevilles completely by surprise. The local anarchy that resulted was to have far-reaching effects, especially when the most menacing of the Percy 'pride of lions' was let loose on his unsuspecting prey.

Born in 1422, Thomas Percy, Lord Egremont, epitomised the problem of a younger son with no lucrative heiress to enhance his wealth and status. The result was that he had become a burden on his father's estates with little or no chance of advancement. Wild, troublesome and violent, Egremont was nonetheless determined to shake off his father's yoke by setting himself on a course of reckless self-aggrandisement, similar to that pursued by his grandfather, Hotspur, at the turn of the century. Soon after returning home from the war with Scotland, he began to assemble a band of ruffians to hasten conflict with the Nevilles, and to further annoy the younger members of Salisbury's family he began to distribute his livery of red and black to any man who was willing to help him.

In direct opposition to the Nevilles' authority in the West March, Egremont soon set up his headquarters at Cockermouth, and in 1447 he and his retainers rode south into Neville territory, the result being that he was flung into York gaol for disturbing the peace. When he was released, on two separate occasions, both feuding families deliberately ignored summonses by the king to muster for service in France in favour of challenging each other's interests in Yorkshire. Not surprisingly, Sir John Neville, Salisbury's younger son, rose to Egremont's bait, and in 1453 he raided the Percy lordship of Topcliffe, on the pretext of apprehending his opposite number. In reply, Sir Richard Percy, Egremont's brother, attacked the Neville manors of Halton and Swinden, and the resulting spate of raiding caused a complete breakdown of law and order in the county. Troublemakers from all over Yorkshire began to abuse the law while the government was impotent and King Henry was insane. However, the next affront to Neville ascendancy was aimed directly at the earl of Salisbury and leading members of his family. In fact, it is more than likely that Egremont intended to assassinate the earl, in a frenzy of bloodletting that would leave the Percys once more in control of the north.

On 24 August 1453, Salisbury, his countess, Sir Thomas Neville and Neville's new bride Maud Stanhope, a niece of Ralph Lord Cromwell, were travelling north from Tattershall Castle in Lincolnshire, where Thomas and Maud had been celebrating their wedding. It was Egremont's intention to stop them beyond the gates of York, and to this end he and Sir Richard Percy succeeded in gathering 700 men to block the road at

Heworth Moor – a route that the Nevilles had to take to reach Sherriff Hutton, one of their many castles in North Yorkshire. Lord Cromwell's willingness to settle the Yorkshire castle of Wressle on the young Neville couple was another affront to the Percy family. Wressle had formerly been a possession of theirs in the reign of Henry IV, and clearly a property that they sought to eventually recover as part of their rehabilitation programme. Doubtless, the earl of Northumberland hoped that the castle would someday be returned to the family by peaceful negotiation, but he clearly did not bargain on two of his sons trying to settle the property dispute by force of arms. The annalist of Whitby Abbey was well placed to report that 'there arose... a great discord betwixt him [Northumberland] and Richard, the Erle of Salisbery hys Wyfe's Brother, insomuch that many men of both partes were beten, slayne, and hurt.'[1]

After the 'battle' at Heworth Moor, a full-scale inquiry was launched into the incident by the duke of York, and therefore an accurate picture of a noble's 'private army' prior to the onset of the Wars of the Roses can be reconstructed. Names, occupations and an indication of where the accused lived are all recorded, while the detailed information gives the distinct impression that Egremont's antagonism towards the Neville family was well supported by Yorkshiremen, who formed ninety-four per cent of his force. Approximately fifteen per cent of the indicted men were freemen and tradesmen from the city of York, and some willing partisans had come from Doncaster, Scarborough and Hull. As might be expected, most of the Percy manors were well represented in Egremont's muster, half of those men named being described as yeomen farmers – some from the Percy honour of Cockermouth, in Cumberland, who had followed Egremont's lead since 1447. Outside the Percy sphere of influence, a handful of sympathisers from Lincolnshire, Westmoreland and Lancashire had decided to join him, while mariners and chapmen had been recruited from Scarborough, Hull and Whitby, the result being that a diverse and largely untrained army was at Egremont's disposal. Clerics also formed part of the Percy muster, and men like Thomas Colvel, vicar of Topcliffe, and William Wood, rector of Leathley, were on hand to provide more spiritual support if it was needed.

Egremont's following my have been ill-disciplined, but it was certainly not an unruly band of thugs spoiling for a fight. The commanders of the 'army' were knights and gentry who were professional soldiers. Most of those named in the indictment were retainers of the earl of

Northumberland, and no doubt Egremont was equally well supplied with esquires and gentlemen who owed their landed interest and hence their lives to his father. However, the purely mercenary decision to assassinate leading members of the Neville family was most likely Egremont's own brainchild, and this is probably why the attack on the Nevilles failed. Although it is recorded that some casualties were sustained before Egremont let the earl of Salisbury and his entourage pass through his ranks, it is not known how serious the confrontation became. It is recorded that Sir William Buckton personally attacked the earl of Salisbury at some point in the skirmishing; therefore, the 'battle' was not an insignificant affair. The Neville wedding party may have been too strong for Percy's liking, or another theory runs that Egremont's men began fighting with the Nevilles only to withdraw for some reason, probably fearing the consequences of their action. Whatever the real reason for the 'battle of Heworth Moor', for the first time in their history Neville and Percy had crossed swords, and this was a situation that the existing government could not tolerate.

Despite vain attempts at mediation between the Nevilles and the Percys, the autumn of 1453 was punctured by several renewed outbursts of violence, each side turning a deaf ear to royal commands and civic pleadings. As far as both sides were concerned, nothing had been settled at Heworth: swords had been drawn, men had confronted each other prepared for war, and property had been ransacked – to no advantage. It may have been irresponsible for Lord Egremont to act so foolishly against the Nevilles, but what if much larger political ideals had prompted the Percys to act so confidently in the first place? In short, had the machinations of Henry Holand, Duke of Exeter, been at work in the north much earlier than historians think?

Earlier that year, Lord Cromwell (Neville's recent benefactor) was involved in a dispute with Lord Grey of Ruthin and Henry Holand, Duke of Exeter, that proved of great importance to how Egremont and the Percys would conduct their war against the Nevilles from then on. Exeter was descended of royal blood, and it is certain that he had ambitions far beyond his means, not to mention his intellect. In 1452, he had claimed two of Cromwell's manors which were also pursued by Lord Grey, who had a similar entitlement to the estates. Grey managed to come to a temporary agreement with Cromwell, but Exeter was not a patient man and he forcibly dispossessed the latter of his manor of Ampthill in Bedfordshire in 1453. This caused another family feud, resulting in a stern reprimand from the Crown and orders to immediately appear before the king. However, when the respective factions finally arrived in London their presence was backed by force, each having armed retinues with which they hoped to overawe the court, and all three men suffered a spell of imprisonment before being dismissed back to their respective estates. No further action was taken, but it was no accident that the browbeaten Exeter later sought out Lord Egremont and the Percys in a bid to topple Cromwell, their common enemy. Proof of this pact was recorded in an official London newsletter, which reported that on 19 January 1454 Lord Egremont and the duke of Exeter swore an oath of allegiance at Tuxford, near Doncaster, to further their aims against the Nevilles and anyone else who opposed them. It was the start of the kind of factionalism that later led to civil war.

The historian G.M. Trevelyan remarked that 'the Wars of the Roses were to a large extent a quarrel between Welsh Marcher Lords, who were also great English nobles, closely related to the English throne'.[2] This opinion was endorsed by Ralph A. Griffiths, but modified by a more valid observation that if Trevelyan had looked northwards, especially to Yorkshire, 'he might well have described the Wars of the Roses as in part a quarrel between great Yorkshire magnates who were also involved in the campaign to reform and ultimately displace the Lancastrian government'.[3] Certainly the opening skirmishes between the Nevilles and the Percys, which culminated in the first battle of St Albans, were the model for all confrontations thereafter. Local feuding and rivalry was a problem that had caused division in the past, and with no forceful king to quell the instability at source this behaviour could only lead to widespread rebellion. In fact, on 20 October 1453, after further risings had been staged in Yorkshire, the northern feud reached a new and dangerous height, for exactly these reasons.

Prior to the official alliance between Lord Egremont and the duke of Exeter, a major battle was almost fought near the Percy manor of Topcliffe in North Yorkshire. With Neville and Percy armies numbered in thousands rather than hundreds, the stage had been set for a bloodbath which might have been described, had it occurred, as the first major battle of the Wars of the Roses. Instead, the battle was called off and both sides agreed to a truce, even though most of the key protagonists had arrived in strength, including the earl of Warwick, who had accompanied his father,

Salisbury, for the first time. Lord Egremont, who had been supported by Henry Lord Poynings and Lord Thomas Clifford of Skipton, was no doubt mortified that the confrontation had once again been inconclusive. As at Heworth, both sides commanded personal armies of well-equipped retainers, tenants and local town militias, similar to those who would later fight in the Wars of the Roses. Indeed, the very fact that the armies at Topcliffe and Heworth were made up of professional soldiers rather than ill-organised ruffians probably caused commanders to dismiss their armies without major bloodshed. In short, the first battle of the Wars of the Roses had merely been postponed to a later date.

With the king incapacitated, it was the duke of York's responsibility, as regent, to put down the northern rebellion, and the massive concentration of Percy strength at Spofforth Castle in Yorkshire on 21 May 1454, not to mention the appearance of the duke of Exeter in the north, prompted York to march from London without delay. However, Exeter and Egremont had already anticipated York's move against them and, after claiming the duchy of Lancaster as his own and distributing liveries of red and white to anyone who would follow him, Exeter embarked on a highly dangerous campaign that directly threatened York's authority. With Egremont at his side, Exeter marched on York, then Hull, in an effort to extend his control over Yorkshire. However, it was an enterprise which was doomed to failure, primarily due to his lack of foresight. Turning west after a failed attempt to seize Hull, the rebels soon dispersed, although a force led by Robert Mauleverer tried to organise opposition against the duke of York when he entered the county. Caught between Duke Richard with an army in the east and Sir Thomas Stanley in the west, Exeter fled to sanctuary at Westminster, where he was advised to submit his 'grievances' directly to the king – undoubtedly a petition that he could not uphold. It was left to York, the Nevilles and the justices of the City of York to conclude the rebellion by indicting the main culprits; by placing the blame on Exeter and the Percys, the Nevilles moved one step closer to an alliance with the Protector.

It is not surprising that when the duke of York returned to London on 4 July 1454 one of his first tasks was to have Exeter and his bastard brother, Robert, forcibly removed from sanctuary. Immediately conveyed into the north, the renegade duke was imprisoned in Pontefract Castle, where the earl of Salisbury was tasked to keep a watchful eye on him. As a further punishment, Exeter's claimed manors of Ampthill and

Fanhope, fought over so vehemently with Lord Cromwell, were granted to Lord Grey of Ruthin. It seemed as if the northern rebellion had been defeated. However, Exeter's accomplice was not deterred, and in October 1454 Lord Egremont decided to attack the Neville manor of Stamford Bridge near York, in the hope of renewing the conflict. The *Whitby Cartulary* recorded the disaster which befell the Percys when Egremont and his brother Richard Percy, along with 200 Pocklington men, clashed with Sir Thomas and Sir John Neville. At some point during the raid, the bailiff of Pocklington, Peter Lound, fled with his men, leaving Egremont at the Nevilles' mercy. It was to be the end of the Percys' reign of terror in the north. Unable to pay the vast sum of money owed to the Nevilles in damages (16,800 marks), Egremont was first conveyed to Middleham Castle then to London, where he was imprisoned in Newgate prison for the next two years.

Disorder in the north and the recent disasters in France were probably the main causes of the king's breakdown in August 1453. However, when the duke of York was dismissed as Protector in 1454, the speed at which his enemy Somerset was restored to power was a move on the part of King Henry that was bound to cause a renewed sense of anxiety in the 'Yorkist' camp. The correctness of discharging York from his duties can be understood, but the blatant and imprudent restoration of a hated former minister, rather than the transfer of authority to a third party, smacks of an unscrupulous guiding hand behind the throne. York certainly knew that, once released, Somerset would seek his elimination from politics as quickly as possible. Only this, and the establishment of a new government, could ensure Somerset's survival. York's rival undoubtedly knew that if ever the king had another relapse of his debilitating illness then the same incarceration process, or worse, might befall him if York assumed the Protectorship indefinitely.

It would be imprudent to say that York and the Nevilles had not already begun to anticipate what possible moves might be made against them if ever Somerset was released from imprisonment. However, when the duke was conducted from the Tower on 5 February 1455 York, Salisbury and Warwick seemed manifestly unaware what measures had been put in place to ensure Somerset's return to court. Indeed, York and Salisbury were numbered among the attendees of a Great Council meeting that accompanied Somerset's 'strange' release from confinement, pending his reply to the accusations that had been laid against him. However, it was small consolation to the 'Yorkists' that Somerset promised never again to involve himself in national politics or approach within twenty miles of the king's person. One month later, against all the odds, Somerset's sureties were formally discharged and, far than being constrained, he once again resumed his former place as Henry's chief minister.

Did the duke of York not anticipate this flagrant breach of faith by the king? Evidently not; in fact, soon after resigning his office as Protector at Greenwich it seems as if York and his friends believed that Somerset was actually about to step down from political life. However, the significant change of heart in favour of Somerset that took place on 4 March immediately reversed the fortunes of York and the Nevilles. Evidently, it made them fearful for their lives. The grounds for this sudden apprehension became abundantly clear when two days later, after all charges against Somerset had been dropped, the duke of York was relieved of his captaincy of Calais and Somerset reinstated in his place. Next day, Salisbury resigned the Great Seal to Henry VI, and on 15 March the earl of Wiltshire, who coincidentally had his own grievances against York, was appointed as treasurer. The 'Lancastrian' coup was concluded with the surprising release of the duke of Exeter from Pontefract Castle on 19 March – a development that was bound to cause unease in the Neville camp.

Once again, York was being victimised by a king who had fallen foul of gross manipulation, but who was pulling Henry's strings while Somerset was incarcerated in the Tower? Prior to becoming regent, York assumed that it was only his rival who was labouring about the king for his undoing. But who had arranged for Somerset to be 'straungeley conveied'[4] from the Tower? Who had canvassed 'Lancastrian' support while King Henry was incapacitated? In short, who had everything to lose if York assumed the Protectorship on a more permanent basis? Clearly, Queen Margaret and her son would suffer if the young prince was ever subjected to a long minority under 'Yorkist' rule, and now that York had allies in his personal vendetta against Somerset there was no telling where his ambition might lead. It is no surprise that accusations of manipulation formed part of later Yorkist propaganda, but the question of Margaret's guiding hand behind the throne is inescapable and clearly validated by her later dogged and resourceful involvement in the Wars of the Roses. That the newborn prince had to be protected against any ambitious claimants to the throne was a natural assumption for a

French princess to make, and York was clearly regarded as a threat to the child's succession. Indeed, the fact that Margaret tried to wrest control of the kingdom from the duke of York immediately after the king became insane is clear from one of the *Paston Letters*:

> Item, the Queene hathe made a bille of five articles, desiriyng those articles to be graunted; wherof the first is that she desireth to have the hole reule of this land; the second is that she may make the Chaunceller, the Treasorere, the Prive Seelle, and alle other officers of this land, with shireves and alle other officers that the Kyng shuld make; the third is, that she may yeve alle the biss-hopriches of this land, and alle other benifices longyng to the Kynges yift; the fourth is that she may have suffisant lyvelode assigned hir for the Kyng, and the prince and hir self. But as for the fifth article, I kan nat yit knowe what it is.[5]

According to this, Margaret tried to assume the regency herself, although when she was forced under York's control she could do nothing more than work secretly for Somerset's release. When Henry showed signs of improvement (though there is no confirmation that the king was ever completely sane again), the support for Somerset was so overwhelming that it is hard to believe that Margaret had not been active behind the scenes. At a Great Council meeting on 5 February, only York was overtly hostile to Somerset's release, which supports the claim that a great deal of work had gone into promoting his freedom.

With the battle lines now drawn in anger – if not in blood – and King Henry once more back under (the queen's) control, only one course of action presented itself to York and his Neville allies: Somerset had to be permanently removed from politics. Having withdrawn into the north, rather than to Ludlow or another of Duke Richard's many English lord-ships, the Yorkists immediately began to muster an army. It is highly likely that this recruitment took place in and around Sandal Castle, near Wakefield, and at Middleham, one of the Nevilles' premier castles in Yorkshire. The court party apparently had no idea of Yorkist preparations at this time, but after the dispersal of York and the Nevilles from London on 7 March it is plausible that Somerset and his supporters immediately set about closing ranks around the king, forming an inner council that much resembled the buttress to Henry's throne that had existed in the 1440s.

But was anyone prepared for civil war? Clearly the court party was dilatory, and saw the abrupt disappearance of the Yorkists as more of a political problem rather than a military threat. Instead of a swift campaign to rid the kingdom of 'northern' discontent, the official reaction was to summon a council at Leicester, the declared purpose being to provide for the personal safety of the king and the Prince of Wales. Messengers were sent out to various shires, carrying letters bidding only certain lords and knights to attend the meeting. However, York and the Nevilles were not excluded from the Leicester council; therefore it is assumed that the Yorkist lords must have been immediately alerted to the very real danger of either being exposed as traitors or, worse, being sought out and assassinated by their enemies. Proof of a plot to undermine the Yorkist lords at Leicester was later confirmed when news reached them that another covert meeting had taken place previously, at Westminster, soon after they had left London, and to which neither York nor his allies had been invited. In a letter written by York, Salisbury and Warwick to the chancellor, Archbishop Bourchier, on 20 May 1455, immediately prior to the battle of St Albans, the reference to a secret meeting is abundantly clear. Their 'mistrust to somme persones'[6] is a feature of the suspicions that York and the Neville must have felt at this time, and the main reason why they set about protecting themselves both by mustering men and by preparing the petitions of loyalty that they hoped to put before the king.

As it transpired, the Leicester council never met, due to the ensuing battle of St Albans, but its formulation was clearly intended to wound York and perhaps even designed to force him (yet again) into acting inappropriately. The royalist lords and knights may even have been brought together in order to witness yet another humiliating scene of York swearing oaths of loyalty to Henry, similar to the aftermath of Dartford. However, it is clear that both York and Somerset had already decided what action should be taken and, although the royal reaction was somewhat remiss, the Yorkists had clearly made up their minds to capture Somerset before the Leicester meeting could take place.

While York and the Nevilles were recruiting their forces in the north, there was an element of unrest in the south, leading us to believe that Somerset, at least, was preparing for a hostile reaction to his release. According to the Dijon Relation, he had become extremely unpopular in London and, fearing that the journey north to Leicester might prove hazardous to his person, he set about making plans to protect the king (and himself) from further molestation. Both the Dijon Relation and a letter to the archbishop of Ravenna in the *Calendar of State Papers in Milan* allude to the fact that the royalists were fearful of what York might do next in order to regain authority.

> When the Duke of Somerset and those who were of his party then being in the City of London, heard that the Duke of York and many other lords in his company were advancing against them with a force of five thousand men, and when he considered what he had done against the Duke of York and that he was also in very bad odour with the people of London, he came to the conclusion that he should not remain in the City of London for fear that the people would fall on him the moment he [York] arrived. For which cause he persuaded the king to sally forth against the said Duke of York and his other enemies.[7]

This threat of personal danger caused Somerset, as constable, to immediately send out summonses for military help in the king's name, although he must have known that to recruit substantially would be an impossible task, given the timing of the meeting at Leicester. However, commissions to raise troops were dispatched from Westminster on 18 May, and it is highly likely that all these hastily raised contingents were called upon to concentrate on St Albans, although the wording of the document alludes to an immediate convergence upon the king's person, wherever he might be.

The Coventry summons for military support may be typical of what was expected of both town militia and noble retinues at the time. The urgency to send forces to 'wheresoever we may be in all hast possibull'[8] is a clear indication that Somerset was desperate for support from almost anywhere in the kingdom, although on receipt of this letter the exact location of the intended concentration may have been divulged by word of mouth. The council of Coventry, for example, resolved that 100 men should 'be made redy in all haste posibull to go to our soverenne lorde to Sent Albones and to abyde with hym and to do hym service'.[9] Other noble retinues, including those commanded by the duke of Norfolk, the earls of Oxford and Shrewsbury, Lord Cromwell and Sir Thomas Stanley, were also summoned at roughly the same time. However, it appears that these summonses were either not acted upon speedily enough to meet

Somerset's demands or not heeded purposefully, due to wavering loyalties. The question may also be asked: did the royalists know where York and the Nevilles were at this time? And, if this was common knowledge, can Somerset and his council be held guilty of gross negligence?

It is known that emissaries from King Henry had been sent north to the duke of York soon after his party had quit London. Since this deputation included such worthies as the bishop of Coventry, the earl of Worcester and the prior of St John's, it can be assumed that York's approximate location must have been known to someone in authority. Indeed, the official attitude to the abrupt disappearance of York and the Nevilles from court was highly charged and wholly in keeping with Somerset's worst fears. If the Dartford affair had caused Somerset not to worry unduly, the circumstances that now presented themselves were enough to cause panic, given that York now had Neville backing. Warned of this threat, on 19 May the chancellor, Thomas Bourchier, was directed to prepare letters addressed to the dukes of York and Norfolk and the earls of Warwick and Salisbury, forbidding them to illegally array the king's subjects. York was ordered to dismiss all but 200 followers, as befitting his position, and all the other named lords were restricted to 160 each, upon risk of forfeiture. Evidently, Somerset was taking what precautions he could at such short notice, using the king's council to issue the necessary documents. However, the duke of Buckingham (who was to replace Somerset as constable at the king's request, immediately prior to the battle of St Albans) thought the Yorkist threat not overtly hostile, and this later apathetic reaction may have been at work much earlier. As the senior commander of what soon would transform itself from a king's household into a royal army, Buckingham may have thought that Somerset's urgent letters of 18 May to recruit far and wide were slightly paranoid. How wrong he was. The Yorkists were at that moment marching south with an army of northerners, hell-bent on Somerset's capture.

The evidence for the Yorkist march south is imprecise but, like all other medieval marches and recruitment drives, its course is peppered with correspondence and therefore it can be traced by where messages were initially drafted. While the king and his household were still preparing to leave Westminster, the Yorkists had already gained a great deal of ground; hence an element of surprise was achieved. In only a few days they had mustered their northern contingents and marched down the Great North Road to Royston. Here, on 20 May, York, Warwick and

Salisbury signed and sealed a letter to the chancellor, Thomas Bourchier (then archbishop of Canterbury), that not only protested their continued loyalty towards the king, but also declared that they had brought a company of armed followers expressly for the king's protection. Couched in dutiful and loyal language, they also stated to the chancellor that he, in his official capacity of archbishop, should publicly excommunicate at St Paul's Cross all those who intended harm towards the king. Protesting that they had received no invitation to the recent Westminster council, the Yorkists also questioned the summoning of another council at Leicester and asked why it was convened to provide for the king's 'suertee'. If the council mistrusted 'somme persones', the Yorkists demanded to know who had inspired the king with such mistrust in the first place. The signatories explained that their 'lordes, knyghtes, squires and all other people being with us'[10] wished the chancellor to deliver their message to the king, asking that another council, of their own choosing, be convened, where in return they would undertake to do nothing to solve their private quarrels without proper consent. Bourchier was also asked to plead their cause with the king, and instructed to do his duty if he wished to avoid responsibility for anything 'inconvenient' that might result out of failure to represent the Yorkists fairly. Considering that his brother Henry, Viscount Bourchier, and the latter's son were probably among York's followers encamped at Royston, the anxious chancellor had no choice but to act as truly and as swiftly as possible.

It has never been fully explained why the king never received the above communiqué and why the premier prelate of England did not act personally on receiving the letter when expressly asked to do so. However, when the Yorkist proposal eventually arrived at Westminster on 21 May the court had already left on its progress north, and therefore the chancellor was forced to dispatch a rider after them. This courier was Sir John Say, keeper of the Privy Palace of Westminster and squire of the body to the duke of York, who intercepted the royal progress at Kilburn, four miles distant. At 10 a.m. he handed the letter to a royal secretary, Thomas Manning, but aside from this fact it is not certain who then received it. It is probable that it was given to Somerset and that he withheld its contents from the king to protect himself, as claimed by the Yorkists thereafter. The Parliamentary Pardon issued after St Albans, clearing the Yorkist lords from all responsibility for the battle, stated that the king never saw the Yorkist statement and that 'certain persons' were to blame for withholding it. However, aside from exposing the already widespread opinion that York and Somerset were mortal enemies, what other harm could the Yorkist letter have done to Somerset, a man with an already besmirched reputation? Surely by now everyone knew that he and York were enemies? Therefore it is more likely that the dutiful Somerset delivered the letter to King Henry and that nothing whatsoever was concealed from him. It was already well known to the king that the Yorkists posed a threat and that they were marching towards him, that their retinues had been ordered to be culled to a more appropriate level, that their movements south had been anticipated to coincide with the Leicester council, and that the duke of York's prime objective had always been to remove the duke of Somerset from office. In short, nothing sinister can be attributed to Somerset, but what is striking is that the king reserved his opinion on the contents of the letter, and it was this, and similar acts of dilatory behaviour by Henry, that proved to be so disastrous to Somerset's survival at St Albans the next day.

3

Faith, Allegiance and Duty

O n the night of 21 May 1455, the king and his party 'rested at
Watford',[1] while to the north-east the Yorkists continued their
unrelenting march south from Royston to Ware. Indeed, it is
apparent that the duke of York may have already received the depressing
news that his first message, sent to Archbishop Bourchier at Westminster,
had missed the king by only a matter of hours, and that he now had to
rethink his strategy if he was to retain the initiative. To this end, York and
his allies composed another letter to the king, complaining of the, 'amby-
guytees' about their, 'fayth, lygeaunce and dewtee' fraudulently spread by
their enemies, 'under the whynge of your Magestee Royall'.[2] This second
letter, again declaring the loyalty of York and his followers, was immediately dispatched from Ware by courier. The communication bid the king:

...not to plese to geve trust confidence unto the sinistrez, maliciouse, and fraudulent laboures and rapports of our sayd ennemyes unto our coming to your sayd moste noble presence; where unto we beseche humblye that we may be admitted as your liege men, to th'entent to show us the same; wheroff yerstenday we wrote our letters of entent to the right reverent fadre in God, the Archebysshop of Caunterburye, your Chauncellor of England, to be shewed to your sayd Hyghnesse, whereof, fosomoch as we be not acerteyned whethyr our sayd entent be by his fadrehode shewed unto your seyd goode grace or not, we sende thereof unto thys closed a copy of our said letters of our disposicion toward your sayd Hygh Excellence and the honour and weele of the land, whereynne we wolle persevere with the grace of our Lorde.[3]

Like their first letter, this second communiqué should have prompted a reaction from King Henry. Instead, the Yorkists heard nothing with respect to their demands against Somerset nor, more importantly, about the prickly issue of their loyalty – a rebuff that could only have been galling to York's pride. According to the biased Parliamentary Pardon that later absolved the Yorkists from their actions at St Albans, both letters dispatched to the king were concealed by the duke of Somerset and two others, Thomas Thorpe and William Joseph. However, it is far more likely that, firstly, circumstances other than this caused the resounding silence from Henry and, secondly, that the atmosphere in the royal camp had suddenly changed, and this was certainly precipitated by the close proximity of the Yorkist host.

It is recorded that the second letter was carried post-haste from Ware to the king by William Williflete, the duke of York's confessor, and that it was passed to the earl of Devon at 2 a.m. on 22 May. Given the early hour, a reply from the king may not have been possible, but a more likely cause for the king's silence is the fact that Henry had not changed his stance regarding York's remonstrations and that complacency had taken the place of urgency in his mind. However, another matter may have also prompted a dilatory reaction from the king, and this was due to a change of command in the royalist camp. Fearing that the mounting feud between York and Somerset might hinder their progress to Leicester, Henry, either through merit or mismanagement, chose to strip the duke of Somerset of his command and bestow the office of constable on the duke of Buckingham.

Humphrey Stafford was a man particularly well suited for overall command of Henry's 'army', due to the fact that he held the position of constable of England by hereditary right. Before moving on to St Albans, and also before a confrontation with York and his allies, this sudden change of approach therefore marked a revolution in royal policy that is highly fascinating, especially if we consider King Henry's supposed lack of military wisdom. However, in the wake of this decision, it may be safe to assume that the substance of the second Yorkist letter was not concealed or ignored, but acted upon in more ways than one. Either way, the king's progress did not waver, and considering that St Albans was, after all, the planned concentration point of all the king's forces commissioned on 18 May, Buckingham's appointment as commander-in-chief must have brought renewed confidence to those in his company. Somerset, on the other hand, must have felt somewhat distanced and subordinated by Buckingham's new promotion, not to mention highly vulnerable to any advances that York might make against his person.

Meanwhile, York's reaction to the king's approximate whereabouts was characteristic. He had already decided to march west at once to consult with Henry personally. Acting upon news from his scourers and those couriers that had returned from Westminster with news of the king's departure, the Yorkists marched first through Hertford, then Hatfield. According to *Davies' Chronicle*, York's army executed this manoeuvre secretly and, after a day's march, he 'gadered privyly a power of peple and kept thaym covertly in the villages aboute the toune of Seynt Albons',[4] where the king intended to dine that day.

By the late evening of 21 May, both armies were camped within a few miles of each other with the Yorkists, in sight of the great Benedictine abbey of St Alban. But what did the Yorkists hope to gain from their armed demonstration? Did they intend to attack the king's entourage without warning and openly commit treason? If York and the Nevilles did propose violence in order to capture Somerset, how could they control who was attacked in the royal party and who was not? How did they know what calibre of troops were with the king and who commanded the retinues that might ultimately fight against them? Would the king finally listen to York's repetitive claims about Somerset's 'evil' council? On the other hand, if the king failed to release Somerset into York's custody, would his allies be prepared to attack the king on his behalf? Evidently, Somerset had no option but to await his fate. He was not only the reason for York's hatred, but, according to sources, he had also been shunned by the people of London, an unenviable position to be in, to say the least, if he ever meant to return to popular politics. However, Somerset knew that the monarch afforded the best protection in the kingdom, and he was shielded by an array of formidable men at arms and knights of the realm, some of whom were kinsmen of York and the Nevilles. Somerset was also aware that other contingents were marching to his aid, but how sure was he that the king's men would uphold his position if York decided to attack?

To begin with, the king's party that marched the seven miles from Watford to St Albans on the morning of 22 May was in fact not an army at all, in the traditional sense of the word, although it could transform into one if it chose to do so. In essence, the march to Leicester was a royal 'progress', made up of the king's household, his baggage train and the multitude of servants who provided for his every need. Complementing this unwieldy mass of sovereignty, there was also a select group of magnates and gentry, each with their own riding retinues, personal baggage and a number of other servants who were duty bound to accompany their masters on their journeys from place to place. Naturally, these nobles wished to be seen on the right side at the council meeting at Leicester and it is clear that their contingents were not greatly enlarged in accordance with royal proclamations. However, a letter existing in the Milanese state papers, written on 3 June, claims that 'they went armed because they suggested that the Duke of York would also go there with men at arms'.[5] Although royal progresses were generally peaceful affairs of political influence rather than military might, it was generally accepted that armed men accompanied the king. Therefore the above letter, written by an Italian correspondent to the archbishop of Ravenna, suggests normality rather than aggression, and we can be sure that, due to the noticeable absence of archers and large contingents of shire levies, the retinues accompanying the various nobles to Leicester were not more enhanced than usual.

The king's household consisted of his personal court, his entourage, and those who provided for his everyday needs 'above' and 'below' stairs. In 1445, very precise regulations were promulgated in parliament to restrict the numbers included in the king's following, but ordered magnificence was expected in the royal household, and that of Henry VI was no exception. Aside from the plethora of domestic offices, which included the king's stables, mews, kitchen and pantry, along with the 'above'-stairs departments of the chapel, hall, wardrobe, counting house and chamber, Henry's entourage was headed by his confessor (usually a bishop); next came the chamberlain's office, then the keeper of the household, the keeper of the great wardrobe, the household chamberlain, the king's carvers (usually two or three knights of the chamber), the master of the horse, the controller, the cofferer, the dean of the chapel and the royal almoner. Add to this list of offices a whole host of other select esquires and yeomen of the body and of the hall, plus those administrators known as 'sovereigns' who ruled all the household departments, and it is easy to see why the medieval household of the mid-fifteenth century had became the largest single institution in the realm.

The number of knights, squires and yeomen doubled in Henry's fifteen years of personal rule to a staggering 550 by 1451, not counting those who were ordered only to come to court at the five principal feasts of the year. The appointed officers were expected to travel with the king on royal progresses and, if need be, accompany him abroad to war, as they were not merely servants and providers in the traditional sense of the word. Indeed, apart from scribes and churchmen, these men constituted Henry's personal bodyguard: a select company of trained soldiers who had attained their positions through military service to the crown. Men like John Brecknock, controller of the king's household, Sir Richard Harrington, clerk of the household, Roger Morecroft, the king's messenger, Ralph Babthorpe, the king's second sewer, and the lesser servants, such as 'Halyn', the king's porter, 'Gryphet' (Reginald Griffith), the usher of the hall, and 'Harpour' (Thomas Harper), yeoman of the crown, were all probably very close to their sovereign when they fought at St Albans. All were certainly trained in the use of arms, and along with other recognised knights and esquires who also fought at St Albans, every man in Henry's household, without exception, was duty bound to protect the king's royal person. It is therefore no accident that many of Henry's immediate and more personal adherents died in the streets of St Albans on 22 May 1455.

If the king's household was an institution and model for the kingdom, the riding retinues of the nobles mirrored its opulence. In terms of manpower, this mirrored image exceeded the king's magnificence on several occasions during the Wars of the Roses, but generally even peers such as the duke of Somerset and the earl of Northumberland commanded limited personal riding retinues. When transferring their household from one manor to another, there was no need to employ private armies, an act which made a political statement of power to their rivals, not to mention to the king. Unless they were threatened, the reverse was more usual, although at several times during the Wars of the Roses this military façade was made real by augmentation and by calling upon liveried retainers to provide support on the battlefield.

Efforts were made to curb inflated personal retinues on many occasions prior to 1455, and it is doubtful whether the nobles in the king's party had even had the time to recruit any additional troops to supplement their households. The fact that the earl of Northumberland, and others like him, had not expected to fight a battle so far away from his northern powerbase gives credence to the theory that military action, at least at the outset of the march to Leicester, was not expected. Indeed, the fact that the duke of York and his Neville allies had recently been instructed not to exceed a required number of personal followers proves that the united strength of King Henry's party was not enhanced. The evidence that Coventry was instructed to raise a company of men to march south to St Albans cannot be taken as proof that a general commission of array was sent out to raise men prior to the king leaving London. Therefore, we may safely assume that the 2,000 men who eventually fought at St Albans at Henry's behest were made up essentially of the king's household (approximately 500 men), with the remaining manpower being supplied by the nobles and the gentry that accompanied him.

As circumstances would have it, some of these lords and gentry can be identified, due to the fact that their deaths and burials were later recorded at the battle of St Albans. The peer presence is obvious, but to single out other men it is necessary to consult contemporary chronicles, newsletters and personal correspondence for clues. The resulting cross section of nobility provided the nucleus of an archetypical army of the period. However, for the balance of troop types that supplemented the noble's retinues in the Yorkist army there is little or no concrete evidence, apart from the fact that York and Neville contingents would have resembled a conventional medieval (Wars of the Roses) army that was armed with an equal share of bows and bills (and, if sources are to be believed, rudimentary artillery pieces).

That the king's men were ultimately forced into fighting a battle in order to uphold their sovereign's mandate is self-evident, but it is surprising how far from knightly virtue some of these royalist men at arms were prepared to stray in order to preserve their own lives. Two men, the earl of Wiltshire and Sir Phillip Wentworth, were both accused of deserting their posts at St Albans. Others, namely William Lord Fauconberg (Salisbury's brother) and John Lord Berners (a brother of Viscount Bourchier), probably took no part in the battle, while the men of the king's household and other leading nobles fought it out with their relatives in the street. The earl of Devon may also have fought faintly, due to his past allegiance and sympathy to York's cause at Dartford in March 1452. Of the main protagonists, it is clear that the duke of Somerset, the earl of Northumberland and anyone associated with them were the ones who had the most to lose at St Albans. Somerset was undoubtedly York's main target, but, considering that the Nevilles had old scores to settle with the Percys (that were still fresh in their memory), this vendetta had a significant bearing on how the battle of St Albans was ultimately fought.

Of the fathers and sons who were present at the battle, Somerset's son, the earl of Dorset, was seriously wounded during the fighting, and it is known that Ralph Babthorpe and his son were killed according to the Phillipps Relation.[6] Sir Ralph Percy, along with Lord Clifford, a retainer of Northumberland, was also a prime target of the Nevilles in the ensuing battle in St Peter's Street, despite the fact that the very nature of nobility meant that most men on opposite sides were related in some way. Even Humphrey Stafford, Duke of Buckingham, the new military commander of the royal army, was unusually complacent with regard to his Yorkist in-laws. *Giles' Chronicle*, the only Lancastrian source that records events immediately prior to the battle, states that Buckingham disapproved of the first suggestion (probably Somerset's) that the king should stand and fight where they were at Watford, rather than continuing their journey to dine at St Albans. Buckingham defended his proposal to continue on their proposed route, on the grounds that he *knew* the duke of York would prefer to negotiate, rather than fight a battle. Apart from his ties with the Nevilles (he had married Ann Neville in 1424), the confidence with which Buckingham asserted his authority and the trust he placed in York to negotiate is characteristic of a man who genuinely believed that familiarity would save the day – how wrong he was. Probably considered the veteran of the nobles (he was fifty-three in 1455), his belief that York would co-operate, as he did at Dartford in 1452, was doubtless the view of an ill-informed optimist. Buckingham may have had some inside information regarding York's temperament, especially his attitude concerning the sanctity of King Henry's rule, but he obviously did not bargain on York's current mindset and the ambitions of his Neville allies, who were clearly not prepared to stand by and let the Dartford fiasco, or worse, repeat itself.

Like other great nobles of his age, Buckingham would have had a large riding retinue accompanying him, many of whom would have been retained by indenture to 'do him service' in return for money and 'preferment'. Indeed, ninety-nine men from Surrey and Kent were paid 6s 8d a head for being with him at St Albans in 1455. The use of indentures was nothing new in the fifteenth century; indeed, the system had evolved out of the older landed feudal relationship, through the *fief-rente*. Money and mutual need were the crux of an indentured relationship but 'bastard feudalism' (the later form of recruitment by indenture) was slightly different and certainly was not as binding as the *fief-rente*. By the time the *fief-rente* disappeared in England about 1450, retaining was so widespread that the king had to rely on his nobility to raise his armies by contract to fight at home and abroad. Indeed, the use of more efficient non-feudal contractual agreements between the king and his military captains (the nobles), whereby a captain agreed to raise a specified number of troops who would be paid wages ultimately drawn from the royal coffers, was the only way to raise a substantial army. These indentured retainers were usually bound to their masters for life, but were also free to make highly lucrative connections of service with other nobles. Some men were retained purely for household or administrative duties; others gave favour and support in return for livery (usually the noble's livery jacket) and a fee (maintenance for a specific period of time), the latter being the source of a great outcry and danger to the crown. Controls were introduced to curb all forms of livery and maintenance throughout the fifteenth century, but retaining itself was too useful and well-established to be abandoned.

Buckingham's large following was not dissimilar to most fifteenth-century retinues, in that it contained men who had contracted for all kinds of service. For example, the indenture of John Gresley Esq., retained in 1450–51 for £10 during his life, recorded that he should ride with the duke 'this side the sea' with three yeomen, two pages and five horse, and 'beyond the sea' with as many men as the duke should think fit. The wording on most indentures was very similar, but some had modifications, depending on a retainer's status. The subservient nature of the lesser indentured retainer is made clear from the wording – he will provide service 'before all other men' – while the indentures of some knights could include clauses such as the one below:

> The Indenture of retenue of William Feins knight lord Say of Sele for £10 fee during his life out of the revenues of the office of Constable of the Castell of Dover and warden of the five portes and the said lord Say to doe the duke service to fore all other except our soveraigne lord the king and his heires in maner following, viz he shall ride with the duke in all place this side of the see with competent fellowship according to his estate or such as the said duc shall assigne him to doe him service etc.[7]

Lord Saye's primary loyalty to his sovereign ultimately provided the perfect defence, if ever the king called his devotion into question. Considering the circumstances of his father's demise, it is highly likely that Fiennes was particularly astute with regard to his connections. As an asset to Buckingham's retinue, he could reap the rewards of contractual service with a great lord, but only if his lord's actions ran parallel to those of the king.

Evidence of a different kind of service is also seen in the collection of Buckingham's extant indentures taken from the so-called 'Red Book of Caurs Castle'. Probably retained in 1448 at an annual fee of £10, Thomas Edmund was to be ready at all times to ride at Buckingham's side with three horsemen, a yeoman and a page. Similarly commanded to do him service at home and abroad 'afore all other', it is probable that the duke relied on his retainer's invaluable expertise in more ways that one, especially at St Albans when he was injured. Edmund was useful with a different kind of blade on this occasion and, as the duke's personal physician, it is highly likely that after the battle he treated Buckingham's wounds (which, according to the report that found its way into the *Paston Letters,* were potentially life-threatening).

The recruitment of feed retainers has been variously evaluated by historians, and as a force for stability in society bastard feudalism was invaluable to the crown. However, under the weak rule of Henry VI, and as a long-term cause of civil war, some historians have taken a retrograde view of the system. W.H. Dunham in *Lord Hasting's Indentured Retainers* viewed bastard feudalism in a favourable light, obviously leaving room for human inconsistency, while from the other side the system has been called 'a parasite institution... cut off from its natural roots in the soil, and far removed indeed from the atmosphere of responsibility, loyalty and faith'[8] owed by a subject of the king. R.L. Storey in *The End of the House of Lancaster* suggested that if Henry VI had ruled competently the quarrels among English magnates might have been kept within tolerable limits, and Lancaster need not have given way to York in 1461. It is therefore safe to conclude that bastard feudalism did not cause the Wars of the Roses, as some historians have claimed; it only provided the manpower to fight them.

In tracing those who fought at the battle of St Albans, the lists of the royalist dead and wounded give a clear indication that all the named yeomen, esquires and knights were ultimately bound by the connections mentioned above. Thomas Pakington, for example, was the sword-bearer to the earl of Northumberland and thus his personal retainer. Ralph Babthorpe and his son were both members of the king's household, Ralph being constable of Scarborough Castle and sewer (server) to the king. Sir Bertine (Bertram) Entwistle was born in Lancashire and had been appointed viscount of Bricquebec in Normandy, lord of Hambye and bailiff of Cotentin. He was present at the barrier at St Peter's Church when Mowbray herald delivered his final message to the king, and was more than likely retained by Lord Clifford, who in turn was indentured to ride with the earl of Northumberland.

Entwistle is typical of those knights who regarded war as a way to enhance their status. His career can be followed a little further, and it is worthwhile tracing this in order to appreciate what most knights experienced in the 1450s, when the English were finally ousted from France and forced to return home to England, with practically nothing to show for their labours. In Bertram's case, he was already well furnished with property and titles in Normandy when the rot set in. Born in 1396 and knighted at the battle of Agincourt in 1415, he had served in Normandy since 1429 and had fought with the redoubtable English captain John Talbot, Earl of Shrewsbury in France, where he was later captured and held to ransom. To help pay the excessive amount demanded of him when in the hands of the French, it is recorded that he was licensed to sell wool to Calais for his own profit in 1445. However, when Talbot was killed at the battle of Castillion in 1453 and the English were finally expelled from France, Entwistle, like many of his comrades, returned home to find little or no employment in the trade he knew best. Evidently, in Bertram's case, he was not to be made wholly redundant; in fact, he returned to his native Lancashire and Entwistle Hall, where he soon took up service with Lord Clifford, who held lands in Yorkshire and Westmoreland.

Like many of his contemporaries, very little is known of Entwistle's actual daily life but, at the age of fifty-nine in 1455, he was almost certainly looked upon as an experienced soldier who had devoted many years' service to the crown. Indeed, he was one among a good company of veteran knights who were in their fifties and sixties when called upon to travel north to Leicester with the king. The duke of Buckingham, for example, was fifty-three in 1455; William Lord Fauconberg was fifty-four; Lord Audley was fifty-seven; and the earl of Northumberland was probably considered ancient at sixty-three. Sir John Wenlock (later Lord Wenlock) and Lord Dudley, both of whom later became Yorkists and fought for Edward IV, York's eldest son, were also in their fifties. Dudley, among others, was named as the king's standard-bearer during the battle. It is therefore not the case that the royalist army was inexperienced or faint-hearted during the battle. Furnished with the best equipment in Europe and commanding the staunchest of retainers, all willing to die for their masters if need be, the nobles and gentry who augmented the royal 'progress' in 1455 were definitely a force to be reckoned with if they were attacked. They had the power of the throne behind them and were able to strike fear into even the most resolute of subjects by merely displaying the royal standard. In short, it would take an extremely determined man, or a complete fool, to dare contest the king's authority on the battlefield.

What price Yorkist intentions, confronted with such an array of imperial might? The question is difficult to answer when one considers the issue of who commanded the contingents of York's 'northern' army. Even with contemporary letters and chronicles recording the battle to guide us, only a handful of York's captains can be clearly identified. Admittedly, this is due to the fact that St Albans was a Yorkist victory and that their overall casualties were more than likely very low. However, it is essential to document the variation between the contending armies and to show the differing temperaments that existed between the two sides in order to trace the battle. At first glance, this comparison is particularly one-sided and favours the royal army both in terms of equipment and quality of troops, but it is apparent that several other factors suggest that the Yorkist army had a slight edge, and these advantages were noted in contemporary chronicles.

Firstly, on a psychological note, the Yorkist commanders had a point to prove: they verged on the terrible crime of treason if their strategies ran out of control or were taken maliciously by the king. Secondly, feuds existed between the two sides, and personal issues undoubtedly shaped what occurred in the streets of St Albans when fighting actually broke out. Thirdly, the duke of York had already experienced a measure of humiliation in the field and was clearly not about to be dissuaded from displacing his rival Somerset. His admonishments in the council chamber, not to mention his failed coup at Dartford, must have had a serious effect on York's political outlook, and now he no doubt saw himself as the mouthpiece of the 'commons' in more ways than we can ever imagine, or prove conclusively. Lastly, the psyche of the Yorkist soldiers was dissimilar to that of the men in the king's army. The northerners who had marched south from Yorkshire and the borders, who were used to garrison duty, were undoubtedly more than ready (if necessary) to fight for York and the Nevilles without question. However, contrary to the picture painted of Henry's shining professional army ranged against the 'rag-tag' band of moss troopers culled from the north, the real strength of the Yorkist army was not their determination or advantage of numbers, which were admittedly greater and more constant than the king's. According to reports, their disposition as hardened fighters was driven by the fear of overmighty neighbours.

As we have seen, Neville and Percy feuding had not only caused infighting among the nobles and gentry in the north but had also, quite naturally, polarised many tenant farmers and local townsmen who owed them allegiance. Richard of York was the most senior Yorkist commander at St Albans, but at the age of forty-four his 'prudent' brother-in-law, the earl of Salisbury, was ten years older and by far the more influential captain in York's army. With regard to manpower, and the command of their bands of retainers and border levies, it is highly likely that the greater authority was also demanded by Salisbury who, along with his son, the earl of Warwick, had recruited the majority of York's strength from their northern domains. This fact does not, however, belittle the overriding influence of the duke of York, nor does it underestimate his ability to recruit from his own areas of influence, but merely suggests that York's willingness to act was nothing without Neville accord. This political alliance, after all, had made York's army more notable as a fighting unit than at Dartford and, judging by the king's orders to restrict Neville retinues prior to St Albans, it is clear that the duke of Somerset knew the danger of the Neville alliance could prove disastrous to him if ever the two united in the field.

Therefore, if York chose to act militarily it would be with Neville consent. With a host of other more personal issues also burning in Neville minds, the chance to accomplish what they had failed to do in the north against the Percys was probably a good enough reason for Salisbury to accord with York's wishes, under the pretence of freeing the king from the influence of an unjust minister. In short, the overriding feud of Neville against Percy may not have impinged on the will of York to act against Somerset, but instead on the mutual understanding between the Yorkist commanders that they would combat more enemies than one under the smokescreen of a noble cause.

Although the organisation of the Yorkist army is not fully documented by sources, we can identify at least some of those men who accompanied York to St Albans in 1455 and thereby describe what troop types they may have commanded. Aside from the three most senior commanders – York, Salisbury and Warwick – we know that Sir John Neville, Salisbury's other son, was present, given that his long-standing feud with the Percys was ongoing and not yet settled. John Neville was probably more eager than most to renew the conflict with his rivals, and although his brother, the earl of Warwick, had not yet suffered the direct effects of Percy hostility first-hand, it is clear that John and his brother Thomas still harboured a grudge against the Percy family since Lord Egremont's personal attack at Heworth Moor in 1453. Moreover, it is also possible that Sir Thomas Neville may have fought at St Albans, although this cannot be proved. It is certain, however, that Egremont's assassination attempt was still fresh in the mind of the Neville family, and the fact that the earl of Northumberland had stood idly by while his renegade son had not only planned the deed, but also had given him licence to terrorise Neville estates in Yorkshire, adds considerable weight to this theory. Evidently, Salisbury and his sons could not see the folly of continuing their feud with the rest of the Percy family due to an ingrained prejudice on both sides. Chivalric pride had to be upheld, and no doubt the earl of

Warwick felt the same pangs of family hatred for his blood enemies the Percys, although the overriding reason for Warwick's fervent involvement at St Albans was undoubtedly territorial disagreements in other parts of the country.

On 21 July 1453, Henry VI had presided over a meeting to settle the differences between the duke of Somerset and the earl of Warwick, regarding the possession of the lordship of Glamorgan and Morgannock in South Wales. The conflict had arisen due to Henry's willingness to grant Somerset the keeping of these lands, which had been held by Warwick since 1450 as part of the Beauchamp inheritance, through his wife Anne. Due to Henry's mismanagement, Warwick had been forced to hold the principal strongholds there by force of arms against Somerset, who was quite clearly willing to accept his king's munificence whatever the price. The attempt by Somerset to dispossess Warwick and the Nevilles of their rightful inheritance was of course deplorable, but the fact that a loophole had been found and exploited by Somerset caused Warwick to mistrust his rival's intentions on a much broader scale, even to the extent of causing him to side with the duke of York, in an effort to punish his enemy. As a result, the royal meeting of 21 July was a chance for King Henry to make amends. However, the decision of the council to order Warwick to disperse his armed followers and, in view of the dispute, to give the lordships over to Lord Dudley until Henry had decided what proper action should be taken, was a dismal failure. Indeed, there is no evidence that Warwick ever surrendered his lands to Dudley or Somerset and, in this author's opinion, the unsettled quarrel was finally settled in the streets of St Albans, where Warwick had the ideal opportunity to deal with both men at once.

Aside from the Neville contingents, other disgruntled nobles had also decided to join York in his effort to oust Somerset from power. That John Lord Clinton fought with the Yorkists at St Albans is certain, although his death there, according to the *Paston Letters*, is highly unlikely. Clinton, an impoverished Yorkshire magnate who had been induced by an act of royal patronage to sell his claim to the title of Lord Saye in 1448, later fought for the Yorkists at Ludford, the second battle of St Albans and the battle of Towton. His death in 1464 strengthens the claim that he was a staunch Yorkist sympathiser to the last, more than ready to face attainder and, if necessary, death, in order to regain his former reputation.

Edward Brooke, Lord Cobham, also joined York's army, as he had done prior to the Dartford affair in 1452. Indeed, it will be remembered that he and his master, the earl of Devon, had been imprisoned in Berkhamsted Castle for two years for their part in York's failed coup, and although 2,430 other rebels had received pardon for their treasonable actions at Dartford it is likely that Lord Cobham was marked out for special treatment by the king's councillors. The result was that Devon joined the king's army at St Albans and Cobham, his former henchman, sided with York, doubtless nursing a measure of resentment for his incarceration.

The Bourchiers too had decided to follow their cousin York against Somerset. Their family were represented by Henry, Viscount Bourchier, later created the earl of Essex, and his son Humphrey, afterwards Lord Cromwell – although a degree of uncertainty exists about Humphrey's participation in the actual battle. According to the *Paston Letters*, a 'Lord Crumwelle'[9] was in the vicinity of St Albans on 22/23 May 1455, but this must not be confused with the fact that Ralph, the current bearer of the title, and other nobles were advancing on, or in close proximity to, St Albans on the day of the battle. Henry Bourchier had been created viscount in 1446 and was now fifty-one years old. He was married to York's sister Isobel and thus his ties to his brother-in-law's cause were assured, although this recent militancy was founded more on embarrassment than commitment. Even though his own brother, John Lord Berners, was with the king's party, he had probably chosen to adhere to York's cause for a more personal reason. At Dartford, Henry Bourchier had been among the group of nobles and clergy who advised York to negotiate with the king and Somerset, and it will be remembered that on this occasion the duke had been tricked into dispersing his army under the pretence of fair treatment. Bourchier had therefore been party to York's capture and his resulting dressing-down in London, and this was doubtless the reason for his backing at St Albans – Somerset quite clearly being the one who had manufactured the whole Dartford incident.

As for the other leading Yorkist captains at St Albans, we can only hazard a guess as to their identities, on the basis of who was retained by the leading nobles at the time, and who was later rewarded by York after the battle. Regarding the latter, there were precious few rewards after St Albans, due to the likelihood of an act of resumption in the forthcoming parliament, when a list of York's favourites would have created a very bad impression on all those present. In view of this, only six rewards were given out to lesser men which might relate to service there. These men were Sir William Oldhall, York's former speaker and activist, Sir Henry Retford, Sir Thomas Lumley, John Denston esquire, Henry Unton and Robert Burton. However, aside from this disparity it is certain that a good proportion of Neville retainers fought at St Albans, and as regards the earl of Salisbury's men two indentures survive which were still in force in 1455. These concerned Sir Henry Threlkeld, who served with Salisbury in France in 1431 with eight men at arms and twenty-two archers, and Sir Walter Strickland of Sizergh, who, in return for a pension of £6 13s 4d, was retained by Salisbury 'for term of his life, against all folk, saving his allegiance'.[10] Strickland could muster a total of 290 armed men, and was therefore a useful Neville adherent in Westmoreland when it came to harnessing the county's manpower. However, one man, who was most definitely at the battle of St Albans and who can be clearly identified as a retainer of Salisbury, is the largely unsung hero of the battle – Sir Robert Ogle, later Lord Ogle of Bothal, Northumberland.

Although Ogle was raised to the peerage later in his career, his involvement in the battle of St Albans, and especially the winning of it, has been overshadowed by what historians deemed to be a much better 'publicised' move by the earl of Warwick. This misinformation did not help Warwick acquire any immediate honour in his lifetime, but since then historians have credited the great 'kingmaker' with the master stroke that led to the Yorkist victory, instead of identifying who was quite clearly responsible for turning the tide of battle. Born in 1406, therefore aged forty-nine at St Albans, Ogle was descended from a long line of Northumberland gentry, most of whom had devoted their lives to defending the border against the Scots. In 1423 he married Isobel Kirkby and set about forging a career in the northern Marches by replacing John Lord Greystoke as constable of Roxburgh Castle, one of the most important border strongholds and strategic focal points of Scottish 'fay' or pride. The reward for keeping the Scots at bay was especially lucrative and amounted to £1,000 per annum in peacetime and £2,000 per annum if war should occur. Particularly coveted by several other northern lords, any military redeployment to the northern border was highly dangerous. However, the other hazard, apart from the threat of Scottish attack, was the winning and keeping of such official positions and Ogle, like many of his northern neighbours, was keen to extend his offices and landownership. Jealous of the acquisition of property, and eager to obtain more at any price, he was no different from most northern lords of his era, and he soon entered into a landed dispute with Sir William Elmeden at Newcastle. As a result, the two became embroiled in what can only be described as a feud, which in the end merited the nomination of a panel of arbitrators to help resolve the issue. The dispute was still unresolved in 1435 when Sir Ralph Grey replaced Ogle as the keeper of Roxburgh, the latter being appointed to the wardenship of Berwick, which he shared with Grey in 1437. Berwick was another primary focus of Scottish raiding and a highly prized border stronghold, but this appointment proved to be a short-term contract for Ogle and, after serving as the joint warden of the East March in 1438, he appears to have sought a more permanent position within the Neville family, hence his involvement as a retainer of the earl of Salisbury at St Albans.

Despite being constable of a number of other important northern border strongholds, and holding the captaincy of Norham Castle, Ogle had been receiving a fee of £20 from the earl of Salisbury since 1436; therefore he was an obvious choice to captain a contingent at St Albans. His close relationship with the Neville family and especially with Bishop Neville of Durham gives credence to the theory that the '[600] men of the Marchis'[11] he commanded at St Albans were mustered through his official capacity at Norham. As an extremely resourceful border fighter and a competent commander of men, the contribution of Sir Robert Ogle to the winning of St Albans has been lost to history, but it is highly plausible that during the night of 21 May, when the Yorkist army was encamped close to St Albans contemplating what might occur if battle was joined, one Northumbrian knight was already preparing to impress his superiors, no matter what the cost.

4

St Albans

To understand a battle, it is necessary to appreciate the ground over which it was fought. Investigating various battlefield terrain features provides the military historian with vital clues as to how armies manoeuvred, fought, and pursued the strategies envisaged by their commanders. The terrain, whether chosen or happened upon by chance, could be either hazardous or favourable to soldiers once they had begun to move and engage the enemy; therefore the topographical evidence of a battle, linked with contemporary sources and weapon mechanics, fleshes out the history, and in some instances provides the essential corporeal ingredient missing from pure theory.

Colonel A.H. Burne applied his famous Inherent Military Probability (IMP) to a wealth of battle histories in the 1950s, but concentrated more on putting himself into the minds of the rival commanders than on examining the actual topography over which battles were fought. When measured against the information supplied in contemporary chronicles and newsletters, the workings of IMP are nonetheless significant where topographical evidence is lacking. However, IMP is flawed on several counts, simply because Burne's unique twentieth-century understanding of warfare could never be applied to the minds of the historical commanders he studied, or for that matter to the mind of a modern general with a completely different set of rules, aims and values to follow. In short, IMP is just the first of many traps that ensnare the student of medieval warfare in a paradigm of thought. The challenge of understanding how a battle was fought is clearly best met with an open mind and armed with contemporary evidence, given that a battlefield will always have its own unique problems and ambiguities, no matter what method of modern detection is applied to it.

Soldiers and commanders of any era, all anxiously seeking victory (and survival) amid the greatest of war horrors, do not know that a given acreage of land may contain some diabolical surprise, or that the ensuing mad carnage may cause their best-laid plans to falter, due to some unforeseeable ditch, barrier or quagmire. Many such battlefield hazards have ultimately led armies to disaster; all prove conclusively that tactics and strategy in any age are useless against the unknown perils of terrain. For example, how could a medieval commander employ sound tactics in a built-up area such as that which existed at St Albans in 1455, or make his next move decisive if his men were stalled in a waterlogged field or marsh? What were his best chances of communication in wooded or undulating terrain, if his troops were occupied blindly fighting in a maelstrom of flailing weapons and falling arrows? What price their manoeuvrability when surrounded by mounting piles of dead and wounded? How might his captains communicate through the dense fog of war in order to avoid such hazards, not to mention to combat the ever-present threat of fatigue and disorientation experienced in crossing broken ground or ploughed fields in heavy war armour? It is these more physical and largely hidden factors, fused with the practical aspects of terrain, that provide a formidable challenge to the battlefield detective, and prove to all who undertake the challenge that a 'typical' battlefield does not exist, especially if we take into account the diversity of land masses and agriculture throughout the ages. Indeed, the shock of a completely unfamiliar battlefield is the great thrill of the work. Walking the ground and searching the extant sources for clues is the only way to solve the enigma, and this is certainly true of all aspects of the battle of St Albans. Indeed, establishing where and how this particular battle was fought necessitates a complete change in measurement, and therefore it is essential to plot the ground over which the armies moved in order to separate fact from fiction.

In medieval England, rolling countryside, water meadows, ridge and furrow field systems, rivers and tributaries, hills, valleys, wooded escarpments and bleak moorland all denote a particular battle 'zone', or at least this is how we might first envisage it. Two contending armies ordered in three 'battles', or divisions, opposing each other across a terrible no-man's-land and separated by perhaps no more that 300 yards – this is how we have come to view the great battles of the Wars of the Roses. However, the reality of St Albans, the first and by far the most individual of the Wars of the Roses battles, is far from conventional or straightforward, and the *modus operandi* gained from understanding other battles of the same era cannot be applied in this case. In fact, St Albans, according to some historians, was actually a non-battle, a prequel to the wars as a whole and a sideshow to the major battles that followed it. It has even been dubbed a 'short scuffle in a street'[1] by one critic. Evidently, these commentators have not taken into account the fact that no less than 5,000 men were involved in the street-fighting and that a very large proportion of the English nobility were present at the battle, with others either waiting to engage or marching to the king's aid. As we will see in the next chapter, this so-called 'street scuffle' was neither small nor insignificant, and its final phase, resulting in the cold-blooded murder of prominent English nobles, ranks among the most interesting and disastrous events of English medieval history.

Today St Albans is a bustling and historic city boasting a varied architectural heritage, but beneath the modern façade of civic and retail opulence its medieval character is never far away. To begin with, the layout of the modern city follows the medieval blueprint established soon after the construction of its great abbey, now a cathedral, founded by Offa, King of Mercia, in AD 793. However, the origins of St Albans as an urban centre date back much further, to when the Roman city of Verulamium occupied the banks of the river Ver in AD 49. Sacked by Boudicca in AD 61 and burned to the ground during the reign of Antoninus Pius, ancient Verulamium was a thriving centre when Alban, formerly a Roman soldier, was executed for his conversion to

Christianity on the hill overlooking the city, in the third century AD. Alban became the first British martyr, and the Benedictine abbey, built on the spot where he died, soon attained great wealth and power, eventually becoming one of the greatest abbeys in medieval England.

The first Anglo-Saxon abbey was rebuilt in the eleventh century by the Norman abbot Paul de Caen, and the great church soon prompted the birth of a market town outside its precinct walls. Extended and refurbished at various times throughout the medieval period, the abbey achieved a licence to crenellate its walls in 1357, due to the fact that many of the townsfolk of St Albans were its feudal tenants and friction between peasant and churchman was not uncommon. Much to the villeins' consternation, one of their most hated obligations was to be forced to have their corn ground at the abbot's mill and, with few exceptions, the use of domestic hand mills was forbidden. It was an ongoing dispute that was animated by the onset of the Peasants' Revolt in 1381. Thomas Walsingham, the famous monastic chronicler of St Albans, records what occurred in the aftermath:

> William Gryndecobbe, William Cadyndon, John the Barber and other criminals to the number of fifteen were drawn and hanged for riot. Some leading townsmen like Richard, John Garlick, William Berewill and Thomas the Stink, were imprisoned among eighty others whom royal clemency later released. Meanwhile the villeins spitefully accused the abbot, who had risked royal displeasure by his intercessions, of forcing them to join the London mob. Such malice shocked the justicair [Robert Tresilian] who silenced them by asking why the abbot did so. Other slanders about the abbot's reduction of freemen to villeinage, compulsion to use his mill instead of grinding corn at home, and bribing the king were shaking most of the abbey's friends, despite penalties for slander, against the abbot, of hanging for men and burning for women.[2]

After eight days, the king, Richard II, met the claims of the townsmen by sending a commission to see that the abbey's dues were rendered. However, when Richard had considered the disturbances in his kingdom as a whole, and particularly those riots caused by more serious offenders in London, he made the townsmen pay a terrible penance. Firstly, he took the fealty of all the men of Hertfordshire between the ages of fifteen and sixty. Then, when he heard,

...that the bodies of those hanged at St Albans had been audaciously taken from the gallows [and buried] he sent a writ, dated 3 August, to the bailiffs, bidding them to be replaced in chains to hang as long as they lasted. This reduced to a revolting slavery the freedom-loving revolutionaries of St Albans, for none would do the work for them and with their own hands they had to hang up their fellow citizens whose decomposing bodies were full of maggots and stank.[3]

As for the beleaguered position of the abbey, the friction between villein and monk had two interrelated results: firstly, it made the friendship of influential people outside the abbey precincts hugely important, and secondly, it increased the abbey's burden of debt. Benefactors were anxiously sought out, and because St Albans Abbey was also a centre of intellectual activity the works of art and literature produced within its confines vividly illuminated the ebb and flow of English politics.

Matthew Paris, Thomas Walsingham and John Whethamstede all exalt moral and social values in their histories, while at the same time aiming to please a variety of wealthy benefactors with carefully chosen flourishes of propaganda. While the recurrent theme in Matthew Paris' chronicles was the wickedness of all enemies of St Albans, Thomas Walsingham was more preoccupied with the abbey's friends and patrons. His chronicles were strongly biased in favour of these friends, and the divine intervention of God in all earthly matters was never too far away. However, the florid and rhetorical narrative of John Whethamstede (*alias* Bostock) is far more difficult to pin down. His boastful wordplay, set in a world of classical and biblical comparisons, gives the modern reader little strategic gloss to the battle fought not a hundred yards from the abbey gate, although without his personal history both battles of St Albans would be a dull set of newsworthy facts.

The date when John Whethamstede, son of Hugh and Margaret Bostock of Wheathampstead in Hertfordshire, professed at St Albans is unknown, but it was certainly before the death of Thomas Walsingham in 1422. After studying at Oxford, he became abbot of St Albans in 1420, a position which he held for twenty years. In 1452 he was again elected abbot and ruled until his death in 1465, his chief historical works being two Registers, one for each of his abbatiates, which he wrote exclusively in order to record his own acts and present them in as favourable a light as possible. This justification of his personal life is such a feature of Whethamstede's writings that a measure of caution must be applied when using his work as source material, although certain local facts contained in his writings can certainly be corroborated. As a friend of Humphrey, Duke of Gloucester, Whethamstede not only benefited from royal contact with a wide circle of friends and scholars engaged in classical studies, but he was also favoured by the duke's patronage. His flowery style of writing, boastful but elegant prose technique, his fondness for puns and biblical rhetoric, and his preoccupation with pleasing his benefactors, portray a man who did not write factual history, but instead wrote chiefly to persuade the reader to accept his own idealised view of people and events. In general, Whethamstede's sympathies were with the Yorkists and his eulogy on Humphrey, Duke of Gloucester, inserted in his register for 1455, gives credibility to the enthusiastic support of Richard, Duke of York. He points an accusing finger at the duke of Somerset for ousting York from the governorship of Normandy and notes with approval the duke's attempted negotiation for peace before the battle of St Albans. However, Whethamstede tempers this remark by straddling both sides of the fence. Since he abhors the Yorkist plundering of the town after the battle in 1455, and states that York's vendetta against Somerset was morally wrong, it is clear that Whethamstede cannot be trusted on certain points. His admiration of Henry VI as a person is also intensified by a certain disapproval of him as a ruler and military commander. Henry was too gullible and easily led by his evil councillors, and this, according to Whethamstede, had brought about the demise and murder of his benefactor and friend, Humphrey, Duke of Gloucester, in 1447. In short, Whethamstede's work is tarnished with a portion of egotism and self-preservation, and it is therefore only useful to illuminate the battle of St Albans where other sources fail to deliver.

Apart from his digressions, Whethamstede knew St Albans intimately. As will be shown in a later chapter, he convened with the duke of York immediately after the battle had ended, and therefore it is likely that he did not actually witness the more violent events that took place prior to his arrival, in the bloodstained streets he described so vividly. Local tradition claiming that he viewed the battle from the abbey gatehouse or its church tower is unfounded, and this is clearly shown in his statement that the king and his retinue kept well clear of the abbey. In this way, Whethamstede states, his beloved enclave was saved from pillage;

if anything, these opinions and digressions point to the possibility that prior to the battle the main Lancastrian position was actually much further north and closer to St Peter's Church than previously thought. No doubt Whethamstede was shocked by the carnage he saw in his home town after the battle and may have felt so helpless amid the violence (and murder) committed there that he was unusually silent about many of the more salient aspects of the encounter. In fact, while the battle was being fought he was probably tucked away in the confines of his abbey awaiting news of events. Evidently, he abhorred what occurred in the streets of St Albans, and he certainly took a different view on Yorkist politics thereafter. By criticising the duke of York five years later for aspiring to the crown, calling it a sin of pride and charging the duke with perjury because he had sworn to reform the government and not to usurp the throne, Whethamstede shows an avid will to survive amid the ever-changing political climate of the Wars of the Roses.

It is disappointing that Whethamstede's view of the first battle of St Albans cannot be exactly defined but, with the help of ancient documents, archaeology, cartography and modern survey methods, the medieval town he knew can be mapped out with great accuracy. However, due to the wealth of information available on the subject, we will only concern ourselves with the eastern part of St Albans and those areas that have a direct link with the battle. This locale can be narrowed down even further to describe the main roads into the town, the streets that converged on the marketplace, the buildings defining the eastern approaches, the 'town backsides', and the boundary field systems which bordered the Tonman Ditch. In this case, conventional descriptions of battlefield terrain are not applicable, and it is apparent that man-made features must be examined in order to trace the movements of the opposing armies. Field names play a significant role in defining the initial positions of the Yorkist army, but houses, inns, ditches, barriers, narrow streets and lanes will denote the killing zone. Similarly, the movements of the opposing forces cannot be traced by hundreds of yards but in some cases by only a few paces. Troop movements will be explained under very limited conditions – essentially, by the confined spaces between buildings and man-made objects. Major changes in the battle will be described by concealed marches through back gardens, attacks across barricades and more covert manoeuvres judged by line of sight – conditions that would never have been present in a more conventional medieval pitched battle. Indeed, both the street battles of St Albans are unique to English history and the first, although smaller both in both size and area, ranks more importantly than the second.

The medieval town of St Albans was originally built on the south-western extremity of a ridge that was, and is today, quite noticeably steeper in those areas falling away towards the river Ver and its extension, the Holywell stream. If approached from the east, however, the ground rises more gently, and it is comparatively level where the first battle of St Albans was fought. In 1455, the abbey, with its great rectangular tower crowned with a spire, would have soared more magnificently over the clusters of half-timbered houses that swept back and forth along the main thoroughfares of the town. The outstretched arms of humble tene-ments and grander manor houses hugged the main streets and fanned out north, south and west of the marketplace, which was roughly trian-gular in shape and could be pinpointed by a relatively new clock tower, built between the years 1403–12. The abbey complex, with its great gate-house and inner cloisters, was sealed off from the 'rebellious' town by a high precinct wall, while priories, religious houses and parish churches dotted both the town and the surrounding countryside. Between dense woods and open pasture accommodating grazing livestock, a number of fishponds broke the lazy continuity of the river, and these yielded fish and eels for the abbey kitchens. A multitude of inns provided accom-modation and hospitality for those travellers who saw St Albans not only as a religious centre, but also as a staging post on their journeys from London. At the heart of the town, the marketplace was a bustle of activ-ity: human cries, animal noises and pungent aromas of foodstuffs rose from both stalls and permanent shops. Square banners of fulled cloth could be seen hanging out to dry in the 'tentergrounds' south of the town, close by its many water mills. All these and far stranger sights would have been familiar to both the medieval visitor and the residents of the town on that fateful morning in May 1455. What can hardly have been anticipated by the populace, however, was the appearance of two 'armies' converging on the town: a far cry from the intentions of pilgrims who on a regular basis trudged their weary way towards St Alban's shrine and sought absolution for their sins.

Doubtless that morning Henry VI, accompanied by his entourage of nobles and their retinues, crossed the river, known in the fifteenth cen-tury as the Halywell stream, over Holywell Bridge (built in 1143). After being appraised of the Yorkist position in Key Field, they would have ridden into the town proper up the incline known as Holywell Hill or Halywell Street, both variants of the word *haly*, denoting 'holy' – the traditional site of a shrine or well, now lost to antiquity. Holywell Hill was the principal artery into St Albans after Watling Street (the Roman road into Verulamium) had been diverted by Abbot Ulsinus in about AD 860–70, and from the river it was lined with houses and numerous inns on both sides of the street. On its western side, these dwellings were bounded to the rear by the abbey precinct wall, broken by the Holywell Gate, while to the east the houses were backed by numerous gardens and fields. Halfway up the incline into the town, again on the eastern side, Sopwell Lane, a road that was similarly lined with buildings and inns, formed a junction with Holywell Hill and eventually turned south-east to form the London road. This same road led to the priory of St Mary, which Matthew Paris recorded as being founded in the twelfth century. However, with regard to the battle of St Albans, Sopwell Lane marked the first of three entry points into the town from the east and was thus of critical importance to its defence.

To the north of the aforesaid lane, all the medieval gardens and properties on the east side of Holywell Hill had medieval strip fields to their rear. These gardens and orchards were bordered by what was then known as the Houndspath, a track (previously thought to have been an early defensive ditch) that ran parallel to Holywell Hill and St Peter's Street. However, the strip fields and allotments that extended eastward from this path continued to the borough boundary and the defensive entrenchment known as the Towneman (or Monk's) Ditch, beyond where larger fields were recorded on Benjamin Hare's 1634 map of the town. Although it is not known whether the Tonman Ditch defences were substantial in 1455, it is recorded that in a survey of 1327 a town ditch did exist, during the Barons' War. A perambulation of St Albans, then said to be without bounds, established that the boundary ran from

Gonnerestone [Gonnerston] to the sheepfold of Kyngesbury [Kingsbury], and thence to the corner of Dounhegge [Down Hedge], and thence to the corner of Tonmandiche [Tonman Ditch], and from thence to the Grange of St Peter, and from thence to Barnatewode [Barnet Wood, Bernards Heath], and from thence to Stone Crouche [Stone Cross], and thence to the corner of the graveyard of St Peter towards the east, and from thence to the Grange of John, son of Richard Baldewyne, and from thence by Tonmandiche to Sopwellelane [Sopwell Lane], and from thence to the croft of John de Hamptone, and from thence to Grenelenehende [Green Lane End], and from thence to Eyewodelane [Eywood Lane], and from thence to Halliwellebrugge [Holywell Bridge] and from thence to Gonnereston by the stream of the river.[4]

Archaeological data points to the fact that the Tonman Ditch was quite substantial at some point during its history, and may have originally been more than ten metres wide and two metres deep in some places. It undoubtedly consisted of a steep-sided entrenchment with an inner bank, interspersed with crossing places that were protected by barriers in order to guard against cavalry attack, and the archaeological evidence indicates that the defences were not insignificant. In fact, a section of the bank excavated and recorded near Key Field shows that the inner bank was more than eleven metres wide. According to the evidence above, the borough boundary of 1327 followed the course of the medieval ditch to some extent, and this entrenchment may have purposely breached the river Ver in the west and the Halywell stream in the east, forcing the waters to flow into its channel. If this conjectural line of the defences can be proved, then this would mean that the Tonman Ditch was almost certainly flooded in at least two places along its course. However, because St Albans occupies rising ground, the presence of water in the remainder of the ditch is highly unlikely. Moreover, in 1427 archery butts were built in what was then called Monkditch, and this again points to the fact that the base was largely a dry defensive earthwork by 1455, which had no other uses.

Certainly, spread out before the Yorkist host then encamped in one of the meadows beyond the Tonman Ditch known as 'the Key Field',[5] there lay large sections of hazardous terrain. Admittedly, many of the duke of York's men had previously fought in France and had undoubt-edly encountered far worse obstacles in siege warfare than urban clutter. However, by the same token, if battle was forced upon them at St Albans then it must be assumed that most of the Yorkist captains knew that the ensuing conflict would ultimately favour the defending army rather than those who made an assault. If the Yorkists took the initiative, their troops would have to first cross the Tonman Ditch and bank, which was bridged and barred in three places by temporary barriers – and which many historians believe to have been guarded by Lancastrian soldiers prior to the Yorkist arrival. The second hazard they would have to take into account was a more general question of which of the narrow roads should be followed to arrive at the centre of the town. As already described, one of the roads that crossed the Tonman Ditch was Sopwell Lane (the medieval London road). To the north of this was Shropshire Lane, now Victoria Street (also known as Long Butts Lane in 1455), and furthest north was another road known as New Lane, now Hatfield Road (also later known as Cock Lane). The latter road entered St Peter's Street by the church of the same name. However, judging by the early occupation of Key Field by the Yorkists, at approximately 7 a.m., it is highly likely that all these roads into the town were occupied at the Tonman Ditch not by Lancastrian soldiers but by Yorkist troops, and thus the defences (such as they were in 1455) were in the hands of the attackers. This obviously made the eastern approaches to the town passable, if highly dangerous, to Yorkist troops, due to the 'funnelling effect' that any bridgehead or road crossing would have had on masses of men with one purpose in mind. Evidently, according to contemporary sources, the earl of Warwick's contingents were not prevented from reaching the houses lining the eastern side of St Peter's Street during the battle; therefore, even allowing for an early occupation of the defences by detachments of Lancastrian soldiers, the Tonman Ditch was almost certainly crossable at some points along its length, and was not as formidable as it had previously been in the Barons' War.

However, more difficult for the Yorkist troops to negotiate were the 'town backsides' and the strip fields beyond the Tonman Ditch. These were more than likely individual plots of land incorporating ridge and furrow, and bounded by dykes, drains and hedges that would have broken up the cohesion of any advancing body of soldiers. Similarly, beyond the secondary track or ditch known as the Houndspath there was a maze of house gardens, and these were obviously a veritable tangle of vegetation, outbuildings and obstacles, dividing up the properties and inns that lined the eastern side of St Peter's Street. That the numerous rows of jettied houses provided a complete defensive cordon around the king's forces and the marketplace is, of course, conjectural. However, it is certain that such dwellings were tightly knitted together, as sources claim that they frustrated the main Yorkist attack. Therefore, apart from some weak points (undoubtedly shored up by the king's men previously), the town, and especially the marketplace, was wholly defensible.

By the same token, any advancing Yorkist troops would have been
screened by the frontages of the houses, and during an attack on the town
it was here, if anywhere, that a breakthrough might be contemplated
and exploited. It was the same story all along the spine of the town, as
far as St Peter's Church at the extreme northern end of St Albans. The
eastern defences and the broken ground beyond the Tonman Ditch were
hazards that any commander with the aim of occupation had to take
into account. It was a problem that could lead to a dangerous stalemate,
where the larger army was only as great as the gap or frontage it tried
to assault. This is precisely what occurred to the Yorkist army, when it
was faced with a blockaded marketplace and only certain areas where
manoeuvrability was possible.

When the king and his entourage reached the top of Holywell Hill
on the morning of the battle, it is clear, according to sources, that there
was no immediate alarm or orders to arm. No doubt a lookout was
ordered to climb the narrow steps to the top of the clock tower in order
to keep a watchful eye on the Yorkist army located in Key Field, 'a crossbow shot'[6] away, but apart from this act of security the king's army was
not embattled immediately. Indeed, most of Henry's men were not 'har-
nessed' (in armour), either before or, to some extent, during the battle.
The clock tower at St Albans is a unique survival of the medieval period;
consisting of five floors, it would have provided the perfect observation
post to view the approaches to the town. The two staircases in the tower,
one entered from the street below and continuing the full height of
the building, and the second running from the ground-floor room and
reaching the second floor before joining the other, allowed its curfew
bell, called *Gabriel*, to be rung and the clock to be maintained separately.
This meant that any attack by the Yorkists from the east would have
been instantly seen and acted upon by the king's men, although at that
particular time, and judging by the attitude of the duke of Buckingham,
nothing was further from their minds.

The shambles (marketplace) below the clock tower was a maze of
structures and stalls which extended from what is now High Street to
the base of St Peter's Street. Embracing an inner labyrinth of wooden
stalls, narrow alleys and some more permanent shops, the market traders
had been encouraged to cram as many diverse products as possible into
one relatively small area. Thus the main triangular plot of lean-to properties and wooden dwellings, which later evolved into today's alleys and

lanes, would have presented a hazard to everyone except the townsfolk about their business. Critically, in 1455 this area would have had a direct effect upon troop movement and have created great problems to those soldiers who chose, or who were forced, to fight there. Central to the marketplace, but at its southern end in front of the clock tower, was situated an Eleanor (or Great) Cross, one of a series of impressive memorials built to commemorate the resting places of Queen Eleanor's body on its journey from Harby, near Nottingham, to Westminster, in 1290. One of twelve monuments erected by order of Edward I, the Queen's Cross at St Albans had become a focal point of the town and clearly served as a place for orators to speak and insurgents to vent their anger on the political and religious matters of the day.

It is clear that most of the inhabitants of St Albans had automatically vacated the town or had chosen to stay indoors during the battle itself. Also, the sight of a large army close by, armed and ready for war, would have been as much of a shock to the local population as it was to the king's host when they arrived in the town. There is no evidence as to whether the Yorkists were actually supplied with food directly from the town. What is recorded, however, is that the Yorkist lords succeeded in keeping their men at a safe distance beyond the boundary of St Albans, and this was to later influence how the armies were positioned, and indeed dictated how the battle began.

Further clues about the topography of St Albans can be found in the *Paston Letters*, which mention that three inns were once situated on the east side of what is now Chequer Street (then an extension of Holywell Hill). These inns were called the Chequer, the (Cross) Keys and the Castle in 1455, and it is these three ancient landmarks which provide the most tangible evidence to link the battle with local history and structural archaeology. In medieval times, much of present-day Chequer Street was known as the Malt Market or Malt Cheaping, with the upper end being designated the Hay Market. The Keys was situated at the top of Holywell Hill, but unfortunately its site has now been obliterated by the London turnpike road. However, the site of the Chequer Inn can be fairly accurately pinpointed, and even though the original inn was demolished and its position renamed several times in its history, its location gives a clue as to where the Yorkist troops broke into St Albans marketplace in 1455. Suffice to say that each of these inns most likely had alleyways leading to its rear, where stables were sited. This evidence survives in more than one location in the modern town, especially at the east side of the present Chequer Street, and also incorporated into the Christopher Inn in French Row. Therefore it is apparent that there were a number of ways an enterprising commander might force his way into the marketplace if any of these were left unguarded or lightly defended.

Beyond the heart of the town, with its marketplace and inns, a broad thoroughfare called St Peter's Street stretched north from the Moot Hall to the parish church of the same name. Between the rows of houses that flanked its perfectly aligned course, it is probable that some of the town's market stalls spilled out into this, and that the aforesaid street was, like the rest of St Albans, not paved in the medieval period, due to the fact that five ponds existed somewhere along its length, the last one being filled in as late as 1849. These ponds were a significant feature of the medieval town, and provided water for animals being sold in the market. Short of any verified documentary evidence to pinpoint the place where King Henry raised his standard, the allusion to a place known as 'Goselowe'[7] (formerly Sandeforde) in the *Paston Letters* may point to a small area in St Peter's Street where the king and his household were positioned prior to their arrival in the marketplace. The lengthy negotiations preceding the battle apparently took place at a barrier located near St Peter's Church; therefore it is safe to assume that the king, accompanied by most of the gentry, was at some point located in St Peter's Street, at a point marked locally by a filled-in water feature (Sandeforde), and not, according to some historians, in the marketplace or opposite Long Butts Lane (Boselawe) – itself a spelling mistake for Goselowe, rightly corrected by C.L. Kingsford in his edition of the *Paston Letters*.

St Peter's Church marked the northern extent of medieval St Albans and, with its extensive grounds and churchyard abutting the top of St Peter's Street, it was the next largest church after the abbey. Significantly, it is mentioned in contemporary documents and local tradition as being the principal burial ground where casualties from both battles of St Albans were interred. The parish church was one of three churches which, according to tradition, were built by Abbot Ulsinus when he laid out the market town in AD 948, and doubtless it was here, rather than at the abbey, that the pious Henry VI convened before the battle. Above St Peter's was a medieval manor house called Hall Place (Edmund Westeby's house), which also has a traditional link with the king, as the place visited by him prior to the battle. Although local tradition cannot be fully corroborated (especially the claim that Henry stayed here the night before the battle, when he was in fact at Watford on the night of 21 May), the above evidence does at least confirm that King Henry was initially much further north of the market area than previously thought. That he did not occupy the marketplace with his troops during negotiations prior to the battle is a feature of the Fastolf Relation mentioned in the next chapter.

At the northern end of the town, at Stone Cross, the road from St Albans eventually turned left from Bowgate to leave the confines of the medieval town below Barnet Wood (now Bernard's Heath). Here, one branch of the road continued to Sandridge and the other turned north-west towards Luton, the latter route being the king's intended line of march to Leicester. If the royal host had not been confronted by the Yorkist army at St Albans, then the itinerary expected and condoned by the duke of Buckingham would no doubt have followed this course. After a few hours' rest (enough time for the king and his entourage to dine), there is every reason to believe that the royal party would have spent the next night, 22 May, at Luton and not at St Albans. Therefore, according to the evidence, it is more likely that it was in the St Peter's Church area, and not in the marketplace, that the king initially 'pygth his baner'[8] immediately prior to the battle, the secondary location of Henry and his household being the site of Goselowe/Sandeforde. According to the evidence, Goselawe could also denote an actual place name, and we may alternatively describe this, as an area (now lost to history), known as Goose Hill, this name being originally derived from the old English *hlaw* meaning hill, mound or tumulus.

It is therefore apparent that after the opposing forces had sighted each other on the morning of 22 May the key areas of occupation were as follows:

The Yorkist Army

1. All of York's contingents were situated in the vicinity of the Key Field to the east of St Albans, and these had been waiting for the king to arrive there since at least 7 a.m. The elevated position of Key Field meant that the Yorkists could view the king's advance towards St Albans, occupy the London road and command the Tonman Ditch defences, such as they were. Clearly the duke of York did not dare order any of his troops into the

town, for fear of them becoming uncontrollable, and this restraining action on the perimeter of the town also gave the appearance that the Yorkists were not deliberately blocking King Henry's path or seeming antagonistic towards his person. There is also a possibility that some of the Yorkist contingents may have been fronted by rudimentary artillery, 'gonnes and other',[9] although there is no evidence this was used to bombard the town.

The King's Army

1. It is clear that the king and his followers had decided to put some distance between themselves and the abbey precincts once they had entered St Albans. At the northern end of the town, and in St Peter's Street, there was ample space to marshal a small army, and it was here and near the parish church that, during negotiations, a 'barrier' was manned by some of the king's troops. According to the evidence, this northerly position was where the various heralds rode to and fro on their missions immediately prior to the battle, and no doubt the king was not very far from these preliminary talks, and a possible escape route if his life was threatened.

2. There is also ample evidence to support the theory that a second division of the king's men was positioned in the marketplace. This detachment deliberately blocked the possibility of a Yorkist advance up St Peter's Street from the south, and it was probably these men who erected the barriers (barricades) across two (possibly three) of the main routes into the centre of the town: namely, at the top of Holywell Hill, and at the junction of Shropshire Lane, near the Castle Inn. Any full-scale advance by the Yorkist army would have been immediately spotted from the clock tower and the curfew bell rung to warn the rest of the army if this position was compromised.

3. Before hostilities commenced, and indeed while the negotiations were still taking place, we are told that some elements of both armies had already begun to skirmish with each other. It is therefore apparent that some contingents were already manoeuvring and taking independent action, with or without their superiors' blessing – clearly the most significant point to discuss when considering how and why the battle of St Albans began. Apparently, some unruly contingents were situated near the Tonman Ditch and in the 'town backsides', with the intention firstly of guarding the approaches to the town and secondly of attacking their opposite numbers.

Without doubt the most overlooked aspect of the battle of St Albans has been the respective arrivals of the opposing armies and consequently the all-important factor of who commanded the defences of the town. However prominent (or insignificant) the Tonman Ditch was in 1455, the fact remains that at least three independent sources claim that the Yorkist army was in the best position to capture these, prior to the arrival of the king's forces later that morning. According to the Stow Relation in the *Paston Letters*, 'the for seyde Duyk of York abydyng in the field aforeseyde [Key Field] frome vii of the clokke in the morn tyl yt was al most x'[10] had obviously arrived at St Albans before the king. The Fastolf Relation has it that 'the king our sovereign lord arrived at the town of St Albans by eleven [or at the earliest nine] in the morning',[11] a notable source, given that this was an eyewitness account. In the Fastolf account, the approach of the duke of York can be taken both ways, but it is most likely that, because the duke had already placed his troops in the vicinity of St Albans on the night of 21 May (according to *Davies' Chronicle*), it was he, and not the king, who was in the better position to advance on the town and capture its defences at first light. The king's march from Watford that morning was timed to co-ordinate with his pre-arranged itinerary of arriving at St Albans in time for dinner. Therefore, since most sources state that the battle began at 10 a.m. and *Davies' Chronicle* reports that the king arrived at 'Saynt Albonys aboute ix. of the clocke',[12] it follows that there was ample time for York to position his troops for whatever action he deemed necessary. C.A.J. Armstrong's pioneering account of the battle also supports the claim that the Yorkist army arrived at St Albans before the king, stating that *Davies' Chronicle*, 'by far the most independent'[13] and 'Lancastrian' account of the battle, correctly asserted that Hertfordshire was a county in which the duke of York enjoyed some influence. Unless an unlikely night march of eight-and-a-half miles was attempted from Watford, it is therefore more probable that the king arrived at St Albans at least two hours after the duke of York. On seeing his bellicose kinsman positioned in Key Field with an army at his back, the duke of Buckingham, as commander of the king's army, then decided to put some distance between him and the rebels, taking up quarters at the northern end of St Peter's Street.

Leaving a detachment of troops in the market area to protect his rear, and placing the remainder of his men at the barrier near St Peter's Church, it is likely that Buckingham (with or without the king's advice) placed the largely demoted duke of Somerset in command of the former. All that now remained was for Buckingham to play for time until the promised royalist reinforcements arrived at St Albans, thus isolating the duke of York and the Nevilles in Key Field. Buckingham's initial plan was undoubtedly to conduct a similar deception to that so successfully employed at Dartford against York, or one that might appeal to his loyalty and frustrate his will to attack, due to overwhelming odds. It was a highly dangerous royal gamble that was destined to fail, due to the double-edged sword of complacency and mistrust, and one whose steely echo would reverberate spasmodically across the rule of five English kings.

5

'I Shall Destroy Them, Every Mother's Son'

The historiography of 'The first "journey" [battle] of Saint Albans'[1] has come down to us through the survival of a number of independent accounts written soon after the event. These newsletters and chronicles were examined and noted by C.A.J. Armstrong in the first comprehensive study of the battle, published in 1960, and were included in the May edition of that year's *Bulletin of the Institute of Historical Research*. Entitled 'Politics and the Battle of St Albans',[2] Armstrong's work provided new insights into the battle and touched upon some of the aspects of its politics not previously covered. As with any groundbreaking research, subsequent accounts of the battle owe much to Armstrong's work. However, in a number of ways my own reassessment of the battle differs from the standard, in that it focuses mainly on the military aspects of the encounter. The resulting research explains why several inconsistencies have been misunderstood and perpetuated by historians, and offers a new scenario concerning the deaths of the duke of Somerset, the earl of Northumberland and Lord Clifford.

Another modern work which embraces the politics of the battle and opens a window into the real reasons behind the violence perpetrated at St Albans is the work of M.A. Hicks. In his 'Propaganda and the First Battle of St Albans', published in *Nottingham Medieval Studies*,[3] Armstrong's celebrated work is taken one stage further, and the possibility of a Yorkist 'cover-up' becomes strikingly obvious. Adding to the loop begun by Armstrong, the work done by Hicks also lends weight to the claim that the battle of St Albans was the first major battle of the Wars of the Roses and not simply a 'scuffle in the street', as previously stated. By bringing the military aspects into greater focus, it is hoped that this present work adds another link to the chain, while at the same time clearing up the ongoing debate of who was personally responsible for causing the battle, who was guilty of initiating the resulting blood feud, which was such a feature of the later civil wars, and, most importantly, why such cold-blooded crimes were covered up by the deliberate falsification of events in official government documents. It is clear that if the truth about the battle had been exposed in the council chamber soon after the encounter at St Albans then the civil wars would have begun much earlier than at the battle of Blore Heath in 1459. Indeed, it is much to the credit of the Lancastrian survivors of St Albans, and the bereaved families of the nobles slain there, that the next bout of hostilities was deferred for so long.

As with any major event in history, there are conflicting accounts of what occurred on Thursday 22 May 1455. Indeed, some carefully prepared propaganda was disseminated, chiefly by the Yorkist government, soon after the battle of St Albans. The subsequent Yorkist smokescreen helped to distort the truth of the matter in favour of the duke of York and his supporters and place the blame for the whole episode squarely on the shoulders of the duke of Somerset and some of his followers. This 'official' Yorkist propaganda was contained in the Parliamentary Pardon, a document enacted at the session of parliament of 9–31 July 1455, the significance of which is fully covered by Armstrong and Hicks in their respective works. Armstrong's opening paragraph of 'Politics and the Battle of St Albans' lists the five other main sources he used in order to trace the events of 22 May:

Battles are the commonest subject matter for news-letters in the later middle ages; and because of the number of news letters reporting the first battle of St Albans it should be the best known of the Wars of the Roses. Taken together these news letters form a substantial body of evidence and require some individual examination. For ease of reference they will be designated arbitrarily as follows: 'Stow Relation', 'Phillipps Relation', 'Letter to the Archbishop of Ravenna', 'Dijon Relation' and 'Fastolf Relation.'[4]

Armstrong goes on to explain in detail these important sources; however, for ease of use and reference, here are the main points and conclusions he made about the cornerstones of his research:

1. *Stow Relation*. Printed by John Stow in 1580, from an original text not greatly dissimilar to a contemporary manuscript among the Stoner papers. The Stow edition has a longer casualty list, and is fuller than the Stoner account regarding the ransoming of the defeated. It is fairly accurate in local detail, but the pamphlet was biased in favour of the Yorkists and sadly its date is not known. However, the last event mentioned is the decision to summon parliament on 9 July, with writs being sealed under the date 26 May 1455; therefore it is contemporary with the battle.

2. *Phillipps Relation*. Published by J. Gairdner in *The Paston Letters* from an original document in the Phillipps collection, now in the British Library. Sent to one of the Paston family, or perhaps to Sir John Fastolf, it favours the Yorkist side, placing the responsibility for the battle on certain individuals around the king, namely, 'The Lord Clyfford. Rauff Percy. Thorpe. Tresham and Josep'.[5] It was written between late Friday evening, 23 May, and the following Thursday, 29 May, the last recorded event being the king's return to London at 6 p.m. on 23 May, with the battle spoken of as taking place on the 'Thursday before'. (Interestingly, the duke of Somerset is not named as one of the 'soleytouriz and causerys of the feld'[6] of St Albans in this account.)

3. *Letter to the Archbishop of Ravenna*. From the *Calendar of State Papers in Milan* and only useful to date the battle and convey the interest felt on the continent regarding the outcome of the feud between the dukes of Somerset and York. However, the postscript, written on 3 June 1455, gives important information regarding the manner of Somerset's death and the reaction of King Henry to the Yorkist pardon. It is dated from Bruges on 31 May 1455.

4. *Dijon Relation*. See translation from original French (Appendix 1). Published by Boudot from a manuscript in the *Archives de la Cote d'Or* at Dijon. This version, described by Armstrong, was a copy of an original finished on Tuesday 27 May (probably in England), as indicated by the allusion to the disappearance of the earl of Wiltshire. It does not trace the developments of the battle from the Yorkist point of view; therefore it may be construed as biased towards the Lancastrian side. Its author is unknown.

5. *Fastolf Relation*. See translation from original French (Appendix 2). An original English newsletter which was in the collection of William Worcester, who served Sir John Fastolf as a secretary and councillor. The letter was written by a servant of Fastolf whom he referred to as 'mon tres honnoure seigneur et maistre'[7] on the reverse of the last sheet. There is no doubt that the author was an eyewitness of events immediately prior to the battle, and his preoccupation with titles and the duties of heralds suggests that he was a pursuivant of Sir John Fastolf, probably attached to Mowbray herald (herald to the duke of Norfolk). It is clear that the newsletter was composed by someone who was with the Yorkist army outside St Albans and who finished writing it somewhere other than the battlefield, given that it contains no details of the actual fighting in the town. The letter also represents the earliest account to leave St Albans and is highly important both with regard to local knowledge and unbiased opinion.

Following on from the earliest contemporary accounts of the battle is the version of events chronicled by John Whethamstede, Abbot of St Albans, who was on the spot to record the battle in his home town. However, as previously stated, Whethamstede was generally unconvincing in his rendering of history and, along with his habit of putting words into the mouths of the protagonists, he probably did not actually see what occurred just outside his precinct walls on the day in question. No doubt Whethamstede played an active, if self-interested, part in the aftermath of the battle, but clearly the important concern from a military standpoint is that the actual battle is not covered by him – although he could have been an eyewitness. As regards other contemporary sources, *Giles' Chronicle*, written between 1450 and 1455, also fails to include the battle from an essentially Lancastrian perspective. As for the remainder of the chronicles, Armstrong only mentions the brief account by Thomas Gascoigne, which was written within three years of the battle.

However, later accounts of St Albans clearly cannot be dismissed out of hand, even though some of these included misinterpretations inherited from the original newsletters written days, and in some cases, hours after the event. In fact, the two chronicles known as *Davies' Chronicle* and *Gregory's Chronicle*, both written before 1471, describe some events during the battle that are not included elsewhere, and the chronicle described by C.L. Kingsford as the *Great Chronicle*, or the *London Chronicle*, contains evidence that clearly states who was responsible for opening the hostilities. The portion of the *London Chronicle* recording 'The ffirst feyld of Seynt Albonys' and dated 'Anno xxxiii.'[8] of King Henry's reign is therefore wholly contemporary with the battle and, although the manuscript was later given its title by another writer (presumably after the second battle was fought in 1461), the details recording the part played by the earl of Warwick are particularly guileless and pro-Lancastrian in tone.

All the above sources contain important clues as to what occurred on the day in question, but the key to unlocking what set of circumstances caused the transition from mediation to violence at St Albans centres more on the personalities, suspicions, persuasions and ambitions of the nobles under York's command. It is clear that two very different aims were pursued by the Yorkists after negotiations prior to the battle were abruptly interrupted, and to follow this situation through we must not place ourselves exclusively within the ranks of York's army camped in the Key Field or alongside the nobles shielding King Henry in the confines of the town, but instead adopt the stance of neutral observers. In short, we must balance the source material, disentangling the facts from not only what was included in the above accounts, but also from what was left out.

We have no way of knowing what the weather was like on Thursday 22 May 1455, but given that none of the letters or chronicles mention adverse conditions we must assume that the morning to early afternoon was clear and temperate. Sunrise was about 4 a.m. at that time of year and it has been documented that the king's host had marched over eight miles to reach St Albans that morning. The Yorkists, on the other hand, had been in position in the Key Field since approximately 7 a.m., and doubtless the 3,000 men under York's command had taken breakfast in camp or in the surrounding countryside. Given the time of the king's arrival, there was no reason why the Tonman Ditch would not have been defended by Yorkist soldiers, although most of these men were more than likely standing down in Key Field waiting for the king and his entourage to appear from the south. It is supposed that the king's men were about to eat once they had reached St Albans, and they must have eaten hastily early that morning or, alternatively, they may have foraged on the march from Watford. In any case, it should be noted that neither side would have gained any great advantage from ingesting more than the other, and doubtless the 2,000 men in the king's host would not have gone hungry while negotiations were taking place.

As regards the Yorkist version of events, the Stow Relation is adamant that once the king arrived in St Albans he 'pighte his baner atte place callid Goselowe in Seint Petier strete, which place afore tyme passed was called Sandeforthe, and commaunded in stronge wise to kepe the wardis and barreres of the same town'.[9] The Phillips Relation also clearly states (with blatant Yorkist gusto) that 'The inony [enemy's] batayle was in the Market-place and the Kynges standard was pight, the kynge beynge present with these Lordes, whos namys folwe.'[10] It is therefore more likely that prior to the negotiations King Henry and his household men were in the open somewhere in St Peter's Street, and that at least some of his men were ordered to guard the approaches to the town as a precautionary measure. As C.A.J. Armstrong noted, the above versions of events are closely linked and may be tarnished with half-truths regarding what was actually said during the negotiations. However, aside from being outwardly hostile towards the 'inony batayle' in the marketplace, the above reports are statements of fact and no doubt authentic. Likewise, the way York marshalled his army in the fields around St Albans can be ascertained. The writer of *Davies' Chronicle* believes York's stance was in no respect passive, in that 'they [the Yorkists] besieged the toune aboute, and sente to the kyng besechyng hym that he wolde sende oute unto theym theyre mortal enemy, Edmond duke of Somerset'.[11]

Given that it was not possible for 2,000 of the king's men to maintain the defence of the whole eastern perimeter of the Tonman Ditch, the above orders given by the king (or Buckingham) indicate that some royal troops were ordered to advance along the approaches to the town towards the waiting Yorkists. In spite of everything, it was not known exactly what York's intentions were, aside from his well-known open hostility towards Somerset. We may therefore ask whether it would have been prudent for the king to appear in any way negligent or submissive when faced with the threat of an army in his midst. In reply to this offensive manoeuvre, the Yorkist soldiers, according to the Fastolf Relation, 'did not enter the town of St Albans, but remained in attendance near the town, within a crossbow's shot'[12] – a clear indication that prior to 10 a.m. the Yorkist contingents were still under orders and had been primarily charged with holding the Tonman Ditch perimeter.

It is at this point during the morning (about 10 a.m.) that a herald was dispatched from the town to the duke of York. Although only the writer of the Fastolf Relation records in detail the names and duties of all the various heralds at St Albans, this information is presented in a uniquely unbiased way, wholly in keeping with a report by a neutral observer. It is also interesting to note how the tone of the dialogue and the seriousness of the situation changes after each successive message is received and dispatched back to its master. If taken one stage further, it is apparent that, on the royalist side at least, political alliances and veiled threats helped intensify the talks considerably, while a conflict of interests and a marked topographical split in the king's forces are exposed to view. Following the Fastolf Relation and using the official dialogue offered in the Stow Relation, it is therefore possible to give a fairly detailed interpretation of what took place before the fighting began. As stated earlier, the Stow Relation was publicised by the Yorkists after the battle of St Albans had been won and it is reminiscent of the Parliamentary Pardon – the Yorkists' official acquittal for what occurred there. However, the remonstrations of the duke of York and the replies from the 'king' are fairly consistent with how other sources[13] viewed York's motives and the fact that the duke never concealed his intention of using force if Somerset was not released into his custody. In the Stow Relation, the tone of the royal replies to York's various demands had to be made to sound both official, on the one hand, and defamatory, on the other, to those (namely Somerset) who the Yorkists said had concealed and perverted their earlier messages. Apart from some leading nobles and those who had become casualties at St Albans, most, including the king himself, were still alive and well after the event; therefore at least the gist of Yorkist propaganda had to sound authentic and not defamatory to the king, or their story of what occurred there would simply not hold water.

The Fastolf Relation includes unique information concerning who conducted the various attempts to avert bloodshed. However, according to the author of the report (Fastolf's pursuivant), then stationed in the Key Field with the Yorkists, it was clearly Somerset who sought to intimidate York first.

> [and] the Duke of Somerset sent Lesparre pursuivant of arms to my lord Duke of Exeter to the said Duke of York, to command him in the name and on behalf of the king, our lord, that he and all his company should quit at once and withdraw, on pain of their allegiance and breach of honour, and all being false to the king, our lord. And as soon as the said pursuivant was gone, once more came before my lord of York, Buckingham the herald, and in his company Joyeulx, pursuivant to my lord of Bonville and they delivered the same message and order as had done pursuivant Lesparre. Thereupon, my lord of York ordered the herald and pursuivant to swear upon their duty, to say and declare to him whether this order was spoken by the king, our lord, himself, and whether they had come upon his explicit orders. And they answered that they had not and that my lord of Buckingham and my lord of Somerset had sent them to say they were coming from before the king our lord having received this order from him. To which my lord answered: 'Tell the king our lord and his cousin Buckingham that I have come here to settle my petitions and requests, and do loyal service to the king, our lord. And if I knew any in my company who would want to act to the contrary, I would punish him myself, as an example to the others.'[14]

Given that the order for the Yorkists to depart was delivered by the pursuivant of the absent duke of Exeter (the latter also known as *Dominus de Sparre*), and given the fact that Exeter had previously been the partner of Lord Egremont (a mortal enemy of the Nevilles), it takes little imagination to conceive that the above exchange of words in Key Field must have been accompanied by much grinding of teeth, especially on behalf of the earls of Warwick and Salisbury. However, aside from the obvious challenge to York and his allies, using both inferred and obvious threats, what occurred next was highly peculiar and lacking co-ordination. Indeed, why did Buckingham herald and Joyeulx (Bonville's pursuivant) arrive before York bearing the same message as before? What caused this strange repetition? No sooner had Lesparre returned to the duke of Somerset than the very same message and order was delivered, yet again, into the Yorkist camp.

Clearly the message had been rehearsed by both Somerset and Buckingham beforehand, but surely it was Buckingham and not Somerset who was in overall command of the king's forces at this time? We must therefore assume that there was either a lack of communication between the two dukes in the town or that, in fact, the two messages were sent out from different locations by mistake.

Given Somerset's dangerous position and previous demotion in favour of Buckingham, the first message sent to York was doubtless an attempt to assert some vestige of his previous authority; after all, neither the writer of the Fastolf Relation nor the duke of York had any idea that Somerset had been replaced. Even York was confused by the similar communications and asked for clarification from the heralds as to whether these were the king's words or those of the lords who were acting on his behalf. Evidently, after hearing the truth, York decided to take an equally threatening measure of his own and bring to Somerset and Buckingham's attention the fact that the Yorkists had reinforcements close at hand. Instead of using his own herald to deliver a message to the king, the duke, according to the Fastolf Relation,

> ...had Mowbray, herald of my lord of Norfolk, called at once and bade him go before the king our lord, to tell him that he commended himself and his noble and good grace, as humbly as any man could do, to his sovereign lord, as well as to all the lords in his company. And he beseeched and implored him, very humbly, that it might please his kind grace to grant him the petitions, requests and demands that he had in the past sent to him, by my lord of Fauconberg and others in his company.[15]

York's humble request to the king was in fact a repetition of his many earlier pleas for justice, used first at Dartford and, more recently, carried to the king by various messengers, including Lord Fauconberg, who were still with the royalists in the town. However, much stronger language was used by the duke in the Stow Relation and, although we must temper this account with the fact that it was clearly Yorkist propaganda, the tone, as pointed out by Armstrong, may be a truthful record of the message that was carried to the king by Mowbray herald.

> *The wordes in writing by the duc of Yorke to the king*
> Please it unto your excellente grace, Richard, duc of yorke, to take hym as

your tewe liegeman and humble subgiet. And to concider and tender at the
reverence of God and in the weye of charite, the trew intente of my coming
and to be good and gracieux soveraigne unto me and alle other youre trewe
liegemen, whiche that with all theire power and mighte wibe redie to lyve
and dye with you in your righte and to do all thin as shall like your magestie
roiall to commaunde us, yif it be to the worship of the croune of Englande
and the welfare of this your noble reaume. Moreover gracieux lorde please it
unto your magestie roiall of your grete goodnes and rightewusnesse tencline
youre will to here and fele the rightwus parte of us your trew subgiettes and
liegemen. First praying and beseching to our soveraigne Criste Ihesus of his
highe and mighty power to geve the vertu of prudence and that throughe the
mediacion and praier of that glorious martir Seint Albane geve you verray
knowledge of oure trowthes, and to knowe thentente of our assembling at
this tyme, for God that is in hevun knowith our intente is rightfull and trewe.
And therefore we praye unto that mighty lorde these wordes, DOMINE
SIS CLIPEUS DEFENCIONIS NOSTRI. Wherfor gracieux lorde please
it your magestie roiall to deliver suche as we wull accuse, and thei tahave
like as thei have deserved, and this done, you to be honorably worshipped as
moost rightfull king and our trewe gouverner. And yif we shulde now at this
tyme be promised, as afore this tyme is not unknowen have bene proyses bro-
kyn which hathe bene full feithefully promised, and theruppon grete othes
sworne, we will not now cease for no suche promises nor othe tyll we have
theyme whiche have deserved detthe, or elles we to dye therfore.[16]

Undoubtedly, the treachery at Dartford and the way Somerset had
manufactured York's submission to the king on that occasion were primary concerns of all those nobles who witnessed the debacle at first
hand, including the Nevilles, who had acted as mediators between the
two parties. However, as York watched Mowbray herald gallop towards
the town and the very same men who had decided his fate at Dartford, it
must have been apparent to all the Yorkist lords that this might become
a repeat performance or, worse, a misrepresentation of their words to
the king. However, the Fastolf Relation is explicit that Duke Richard's
message was delivered to King Henry in person:

After these things being said to the king our lord, by Mowbray herald, he
answered that he had not seen these petitions, and bade him go to my lord
of Buckingham saying that he had entrusted him for this day to give answer

Above: 1 Richard, Duke of York.
Fifteenth-century glass in Cirencester
Church.

Right: 2 Richard III, York's youngest son.
Engraving of a Society of Antiquaries
portrait.

Richard⁵ Rex tertius.

3 Armour of the period. Richard
Beauchamp, Earl of Warwick (d.1439),
taken from his monument in St Mary's
Church, Warwick.

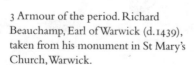

4 Seal of Edmund Beaufort, Duke of Somerset.

Right: 5 Seal of Sir William Oldhall.

Below: 6 Iron breech loading gun and bed similar to the type used in the Wars of the Roses.

Above: 7 Seal of Henry Percy, Earl of Northumberland.

Right: 8 Garter stall plate of Richard Neville, Earl of Salisbury.

9 Mail shirt of the type worn by common soldiers during the Wars of the Roses.

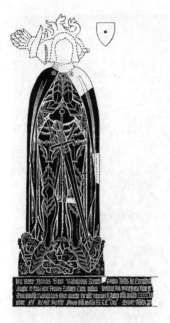

Clockwise from above left:

10 Brass of Ralph, Lord Cromwell, Tattershall, Lincolnshire.

11 Sallet or kettle hat, *c.*1450, made in Italy for export to western Europe.

12 Brass of Sir John Say.

Left: 13 Seal of Humphrey Stafford, Duke of Buckingham.

Below: 14 Long-necked six-pointed rowel spur for the left leg, English, *c.*1460.

Bottom: 15 A medieval army on the march as depicted in the Hausbuch.

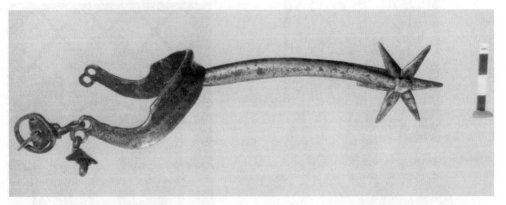

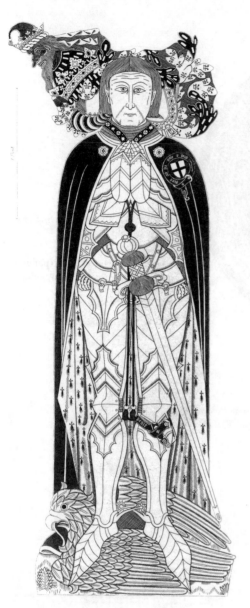

Left: 16 Brass of Henry Bourchier, Earl of Essex, Little Easton Church, Essex.

17 John Denston esquire. Stained glass at Long Melford Church.

Right: 18 Seal of Sir Robert
Ogle, later Lord Ogle.

Below: 19 The great
Benedictine abbey at St Albans.

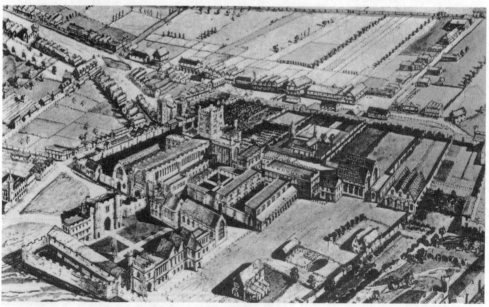

Top: 20 Abbot John Whethamstede.

Above: 21 Reconstruction of the abbey and town of St Albans as it might have looked in the fifteenth century.

Above: 22 Sopwell Lane, looking
east from the junction of Holywell
Hill.

Right: 23 Clock Tower, St Albans.

Left: 24 St Peter's Church, where most of the dead were interred after the battle.

Below: 25 The abbey gatehouse where, traditionally, Abbot Whethamstede viewed the battle.

26 Halberd, fifteenth century, with a single-edged blade.

27 Garter stall plate of William Neville, Lord Fauconberg, who was caught on the side opposing the rest of his family during the battle.

28 Milanese sallet helmet, 1440–
1450.

29 Richard Neville, Earl of Warwick, from a Victorian glass
window at Cardiff Castle.

Right: 30 Composite 'harness', *c.*1453, in the style of Milan, typical of that worn by gentry during the Wars of the Roses.

Below: 31 Fifteenth-century hand-and-a-half sword, possibly English.

Left: 32 Glass depicting the arms of James Butler, Earl of Wiltshire, at Ockwells Manor.

Below: 33 Memorial plaque to the duke of Somerset on the corner of Shropshire Lane and St Peter's Street.

ON THIS SITE STOOD
THE CASTLE INN
BEFORE WHICH
EDMUND BEAUFORT
2ND DUKE OF SOMERSET,
WAS SLAIN DURING
THE 1ST BATTLE OF ST ALBANS
22ND. MAY 1455.

34 An English archer during the Wars of the Roses.

35 Long and short bodkin
arrowheads.

Clockwise from top left: 36 Ballock dagger, 1400–1500, excavated from the Thames.

37 Sir John Wenlock, later Lord Wenlock, who after St Albans became a staunch Yorkist supporter. From a modern glass at St Mary's Church, Luton.

38 The fields below Sandal Castle, where the battle of Wakefield was fought in December 1460.

to all matters that should be answered in his name. Likewise when Mowbray came before my lord of Buckingham and said and declared his full message, my lord of Buckingham answered to him that it was true that the king our lord had not seen these petitions and requests yet and that he himself, would soon show them in diligence to the king, our lord, and would send the answer made to them back to my lord of York by Buckingham herald.[17]

Clearly, according to this important evidence, York's various petitions and requests had not been handed to the king after all, and Buckingham knew that this was the case. However, if this statement was true, and there is no reason to doubt its authenticity, why had York's previous petitions been concealed from the king, and why had York's messengers, including Lord Fauconberg, not persisted in their errand to exonerate his kinsmen from committing treason? Obviously the king *had* seen the petitions, or he would have been so shocked by Mowbray herald's words that he would have instantly questioned their secrecy with Buckingham. In fact Buckingham, and the king, were playing for time. This is doubly evident in his next words to Mowbray herald:

'You will commend me to my brothers-in-law, York and Salisbury, to my nephew Warwick, and his brother Norfolk, in case he should be in their company, as you say he is nearby, that is to say that they can clearly be seen, since the king is present, and they will see his own person and banner on the field, as they withdraw to Barnet or Hatfield, for one night, waiting for some appointment to be made, or one or two men of state and honour to be sent before one to speak with them.' Thereupon the herald asked him, 'My lord, please you bid me something else for this time [?]' and he answered: 'Yes, I want you to commend me to my brother Norfolk and tell him that we are so next of kin that if he had a daughter and I had one, we would not marry each others daughter without a licence from the Pope, and furthermore, he married my sister, that I beseech him to have out of his heart all melancholy thoughts, wrath, and anger for this time, and the king will be grateful to him, and take him into better grace.' This being said, Mowbray herald asked him again: 'My lord, please you bid me more to say before my lords,' and he answered: 'Yes, we want everyone to know that we have come here to support no one, nor for any other cause else, but to be in the company of the king, our lord, as we are rightfully bound to, and as is meet.' Thereupon the herald took his leave and returned before my lord of York to whom he delivered his report, as afore stated.[18]

Buckingham was therefore fearful that the duke of Norfolk and his contingents might arrive in the vicinity at any moment. Given that he had no direct intelligence of this, he wished York to depart and conduct negotiations from a less threatening position, obviously referring to family ties for no other reason than to dissuade Norfolk, via his herald, from supporting the Yorkists. However, the Stow Relation is unique in providing a more forceful royal reply to York's demands, and this pro-Yorkist version of events reveals just as much as it conceals. Interestingly, in this account, the words spoken by the king appear to be from the mouth of an archetypal medieval monarch whose intention was to punish traitors rather than negotiate with them:

Thanswer bi the king to the duc of Yorke

I, king Henry, charge and commaunde that no maner personne of what degre, astate or condicion that ever he be, abide nat but that they avoide the felde and noughte to be so hardy to make resistence ageinste me in myn owne reaume. For I shall knowe what traitor dare be so bolde tareise any people in myn owne lande, wherthroughe I am in grete disease and hevines. Be that feithe I owe unto Seint Edward and unto the crowne of England, I shall destroye hem every moderis sone, And eke they to be hanged, drawen and quartered that maybe takyn aftirwarde of theim inensaumple to make all such traitors to be ware forto make eny rising of people withinne myn owne lande and so traitorously tabide theire king and gouvernor. And for aconclusion, rather thanne they shall have eny lorde that here is with me at this tyme, I shall this day for theire sake in this quarrel my selfe lyve and dye.[19]

Words obviously intended not only to caution the duke of York, but also to strike terror into the hearts of all those men who were prepared to support him.

However, the truth is that the whole of the Stow Relation may be nothing more than Yorkist propaganda, intended to support the story that important messages were concealed from the king by Somerset and his minions. This left the Yorkists with no other course of action but to extract their enemy by force. Either way, their effort to respond to the king 'in person' was proving utterly useless, nerves were obviously reaching breaking point, suspicions were running high in both camps and clearly all York's men were well aware by now that the king's standard was defiantly 'pight' in the town. In short, each man knew that if they attacked they might all be arraigned as traitors. Nonetheless, despite the threat delivered from Buckingham, York was still prepared to negotiate. According to the Fastolf Relation:

…my lord of York immediately sent back Mowbray herald, for a second time, before my lord of Buckingham, begging him to be willing to go before the king our lord in order to get an answer to his requests and petitions. Thereupon my lord of Buckingham answered to the herald that he would with all possible dispatch send his answer by his herald Buckingham, to my lord of York, which he never did. Likewise, because the answer was not sent along, the company of my lord of York was made uneasy, saying, that it was only a delay, which is the reason why my lord of York sent back Mowbray for a third time, before my lord of Buckingham, asking him to answer his petitions, with no more delay. And when Mowbray herald came to the ['barriere', barrier] of the town of St Albans, which is near the town parish church, he found there, Sir Richard Harrington, Bertin Entwistle and John Hanford knights, Breknok squire and John Swythman who asked the herald what he wanted. And he answered that he wanted to speak to my lord of Buckingham. And they said to him that he would instantly speak with him, and they sent him before my lord of Buckingham, who immediately ordered the master of his household and a knight called Sir Thomas Fynderne to go before Mowbray herald. On his arrival Mowbray told him the reason why he had come. Thereupon he returned to my lord of Buckingham and kept the herald waiting till they came back. After going to my lord of Buckingham, he returned before the herald and told him that my lord of Buckingham had been before the king our lord, and was not decided to give them any answer. Thereupon the herald took his leave.[20]

Aside from what was written in the Stow Relation regarding the handing over of Somerset, all of York's frustrations appear to have stemmed from the fact that his petitions and requests were not being delivered to the king in person. He neither knew whether the king was being coerced by Somerset nor whether Buckingham was deliberately stalling for time. Messages had been delivered to York in the king's name, but not from him personally. In fact, on three separate occasions Buckingham had prevented negotiations from proceeding further, and in the end he had even resorted to using other intermediaries acting as go-betweens when Mowbray herald arrived at the town barrier. Buckingham's ill-advised delay and his warnings to both the absent duke of Norfolk and the frustrated duke of York (especially his request that the Yorkists should withdraw their troops to Barnet or Hatfield for the night) must have rankled with the duke's pride. In short, all of the above, and the inference that royalist reinforcements were close at hand, caused York to act more forcefully. The frustration that York must have felt, given that the Dartford affair was still a recent memory, probably left him in no doubt that the king was yet again being intimidated by his councillors. In view of this, there was now only one course of action open to the duke: he must seek out the king personally or risk being charged with treason.

As Mowbray herald returned from the direction of St Peter's Church, 'he found my lord of York and all his company coming towards the town of St Albans and the herald gave the answer to my lord of York. Thereupon [York] replied, "Therefore we must do what we can do."'[21]

6

'A Warwick, A Warwick'

According to the not wholly impartial Dijon Relation, the first battle of St Albans began 'on the stroke of ten hours in the morning'.[1] In the Stow and Phillipps Relations, there is agreement that fighting took place between 11 a.m. and 12 a.m., and in addition to this the Stow Relation states that the duke of York abided in Key Field 'from vii of the day in the mornyng untill it was almoste x of the clok aftir, withoute any stroke smyten on either parte'.[2] Therefore at least one hour prior to the battle cannot be accounted for, and it is this vital hour that holds the key to how the fighting started.

Before 10 a.m. we are told that neither side was involved in any hostilities whatsoever; did some fighting therefore occur between 10 and 11 a.m.? The Dijon Relation claims that it did, and that skirmishing broke out between the two sides while negotiations were taking place. What exactly occurred in the aforesaid missing hour to cause this rise in tempers, and at what point did the actual assault on St Albans begin? Moreover, if skirmishing did occur while both sides were trying to avert bloodshed, was this triggered by some event, or was this armed bickering inevitable?

Evidently, at some stage during that morning there had been a deployment of troops on both sides, not only to capture ground from which an attack might be better launched, but also to occupy areas that might be better defended or from which negotiations might be conducted. No doubt Yorkist levies were, due to their early arrival at St Albans, in command of the Tonman Ditch perimeter and its three eastern crossings: Sopwell Lane, Shropshire Lane and New Lane (Cock Lane). It is also documented that some of the king's men had been ordered to keep both the wards and the barriers of St Albans secure soon after their arrival at 9 a.m. – a move that was clearly mandatory, given the importance of the king's security and the fact that there was a 'rebel' army only a bow shot away from his person. Similarly, there was a third major troop movement that morning towards the northern end of the town and St Peter's Church, prior to the start of the battle, when, according to the Fastolf Relation, Mowbray herald met York advancing in this direction after riding back from his abortive meeting with Buckingham.

On seeing the embattled Yorkists advancing towards him with banners displayed, the writer of the Fastolf Relation probably considered that negotiations were breaking down. However, at this interesting moment his account breaks off and the author vacates the field, not to witness the battle itself. Thereafter we are left to guess what York actually meant by his words 'Therefore we must do what we can do.'[3] Clearly it is a great pity, given the apparent neutrality of the Fastolf account, that York's next move was not witnessed at first hand. Nevertheless, York's advance from Key Field is documented by this important source, and we may be sure that the duke had already decided, prior to Mowbray herald's return, that his attempt to remove Somerset was not going to mimic the Dartford affair. Moreover, given the duke's frustrations, it is clear that this time he meant to seek out the king personally, no matter what this might involve.

But what else had prompted York's impetuous advance? Had a council of war condoned his action beforehand? Were some of the Yorkists still holding the Tonman Ditch while the duke of York advanced his banners towards St Peter's Church? Was York acting irrationally, as he was wont to do later in his career, by deserting his camp in Key Field and seeking out his enemies without a thought for his safety? Or had a concerted attack been planned by the Yorkists from the very start, born out of all the frustrations that had built up over the previous months? Evidently, what must now be considered, in conjunction with all the above evidence, are the actions of the Neville contingents and what, if anything, dictated their strategy while negotiations were taking place. The vital lost hour of that fateful morning in May draws an interesting comparison between the needs of a loyal and conscientious peer and the ambitions of a new breed of 'over-mighty' nobles, bent on survival and local revenge at any price.

Firstly, it will be remembered that there had been a long build-up of mutual antagonism and conflict between the Neville and Percy families, the start of which can be traced back to 1453. This disparity of wealth and power between the two northern houses had caused several major outbreaks of violence, and the younger Percys, in particular, had taken matters into their own hands, culminating in the threatening behaviour of Lord Egremont and Sir Richard Percy who, between them, had sought to single-handedly re-establish a degree of Percy authority in the north. In retaliation, Sir John Neville and his brother Thomas had attacked a number of Percy manors in Yorkshire, and, as a result of the friction between rival retainers, violence and disorder had flared up in several places in the county, causing a sudden collapse of law and order. That Henry's government had failed to curb the disturbances was a travesty and a complete failure on the part of the king and his chief councillors. However, by 1454 the northern conflict had widened to draw in the dukes of York and Exeter, and by January of that year it was apparent that Duke Richard and the Neville earls of Salisbury and Warwick had come together as allies, following the mental collapse of Henry VI and the release from prison of the duke of Somerset. It is also apparent that another private feud between Somerset and Warwick regarding disputed land in Glamorgan had forced the latter to side with York, although prior to this Warwick had also sided against the Percys, his ancestral rivals, at Topcliffe, where a major battle was narrowly avoided. Add to this the fact that the duke of York had also inadvertently sided with the Nevilles against the Percys in an effort to curb northern unrest, indicting the earl of Northumberland, his son Egremont and the duke of Exeter in the process, and it is clear feelings were running high at St Albans in more ways than one.

The two main factions that were to feature so predominantly in the first phase of the Wars of the Roses had been formed long before the first battle of St Albans began, and although, miraculously, northern feuding had remained relatively bloodless, it was probably clear to both sides that nothing had been settled. As fate would have it, the next encounter between the Nevilles and the Percys was in the streets of St Albans. Indeed, according to two important sources, the no-man's-land between the two opposing sides known later as the 'town backsides' was already becoming a 'northern' battleground, where long-standing arguments were being contested. Incredibly, and contrary to York's wishes, skirmishing had broken out here while negotiations were still continuing, and the Dijon Relation is adamant that this armed bickering had started well before the herald from the king (Somerset) had arrived to deliver his first scathing message to the duke of York:

> The reply that was made from the king's side to the said Duke of York was that he [the king] was unaware that there were any traitors about him were it not for the Duke of York himself who had risen against the crown. And even before this reply came to the Duke of York there began a skirmish before the village by one side and the other. And thus when the Duke of York had the aforesaid reply the battle became more violent and both sides with banners displayed began to fight.[4]

The above timings give us the impression that the main battle began soon after two messages had been delivered, one to one side and one to the other, which, according the most authentic version of events described in the Fastolf Relation, was certainly not the case. However, the same preliminary skirmishing is also revealed in an independent English source, which incidentally makes no attempt to conceal the name of the man who instigated it. According to the *London Chronicle*, after his arrival at St Albans the king:

> sent certayn of his lordis desyryng hym [York] to kepe the peas and to departe, but in conclucion while they were tretyng of the peas, The Erle of warwyk with the march men and othir Entyrd the othir Ende of the towne, and ffawgth agayne the kyngis partye.[5]

The fact that the earl of Warwick is named at all with regard to this seemingly unchivalrous behaviour is bad enough. However, the implication that his men then made an assault on the 'kyngis partye' is surely wrong and against York's apparent wish to negotiate the release of Somerset into his custody. If this is true, who made the decision to launch an attack at the other end of the town? What had caused the apparent escalation from skirmishing into an all-out assault, and were both sides drawn into a major conflict by chance or had a co-ordinated attack been planned right from the start?

From a chronicler's point of view, it may not have been possible to distinguish these two modes of warfare, and clearly the timings of Warwick's actions could have been drawn together by the above authors to form a more concise and newsworthy account of the battle at their leisure. Clearly Warwick's command of the assault on the town marks him out as the instigator of the battle, but the skirmishing beforehand had evidently started much earlier, while negotiations were still progressing. However, with both sides in such close proximity it is perhaps not surprising that trouble started, and in this respect the two opposing forces of Neville and Percy certainly had the opportunity, and the willingness, to mark out their local enemies and set about them. Under these circumstances, an escalation of their private feuding would have been too difficult for either side to restrain, both nobles and their retainers quite clearly recognising the fact that here was a battleground on which to right the wrongs of the two previous years of rivalry. The fact that Lesparre, the herald of the hated duke of Exeter, had ominously made his presence known in association with the duke of Somerset probably did not help the situation. Since advertising his authority as Somerset's envoy in the Yorkist camp, it is hardly likely that Warwick welcomed the association of Exeter with Somerset, his enemy in Glamorgan. However, aside from testing York's patience and the Nevilles' powers of restraint, the arrival of Lesparre would no doubt have inadvertently triggered another, far greater concern within the Yorkist command, and this was undoubtedly the real reason why the preliminary skirmishing occurred.

Unlike at Dartford, where York had appeared isolated, at St Albans approximately two-thirds of his army consisted of contingents supplied by the Nevilles. This was clearly a great asset, but also a great drawback, chiefly because the Nevilles and the Percys had now, albeit accidentally,

taken opposing sides. The catalyst undoubtedly caused an unstable pow-
der keg of emotions, and in the end this must have threatened York and
Neville unity. As the various heralds rode back and forth with messages
containing warnings of attainder, veiled threats and delaying tactics, the
Nevilles and Percys were hardly likely to ignore their chequered past, and
the drawing together of both sides' retainers undoubtedly caused their
troops to act impulsively. Therefore the preliminary skirmishing and, ultimately, the main battle that arose from this disunity were as much the result
of the polarisation between the Yorkist commanders as the continuation
of the Neville and Percy feud. However, far from curbing the actions of
his northern allies, York's aim was to capture the king's attention, and this
is why on his last mission Mowbray herald found Duke Richard and his
'battle' advancing towards the northern end of the town. Confident that
the skirmishing before St Albans was now beyond his control, and being
vehemently contested by the Nevilles and Percys, the actions of York, by
comparison, were clearly directed towards protecting the king from the
resulting lawlessness. This undoubtedly left the Nevilles with a free hand
to pursue their feud against their local enemies, and by acting independ-
ently of York's wishes they nearly lost him the battle.

What of the king's men while all this skirmishing was going on? The
duke of Somerset, in particular, was no doubt feeling increasingly isolated by the appointment of Buckingham as constable. However, the
dispatch of separate heralds into the Yorkist camp clearly indicates that
Somerset still enjoyed some influence over the king. Buckingham too,
on York's insistence, spoke on behalf of the king, and we may wonder
whether both these messages were indeed the actual words of the king
or if they instead betrayed the feelings, and the fears, of his two chief
advisors.

Evidently, the roads into St Albans were at some point barred, but
not, according to contemporary accounts, in the way that most historians describe. Indeed, according to three accounts, temporary barricades
were thrown up across the streets as a precaution against attack. We may
conjecture that these barricades had been erected after royalist soldiers
had been ordered to guard the approaches to the town, and undoubtedly
the barriers that Whethamstede mentions were put into position once
skirmishing began. As to where these were erected, there is no historical or topographical evidence, apart from a brief mention in the Fastolf
Relation that one was positioned near St Peter's Church. However, we

may confidently state that, due to what occurred when these barriers were attacked, these obstructions were not contiguous to the Tonman Ditch but instead positioned between the houses at the top of Holywell Hill, across Shropshire Lane, abutting the wall of the Castle Inn, and most likely at the end of New Lane, additionally fortifying a more substantial barrier or gate that was manned by royalist guards further down the road. This latter section of the perimeter was where Mowbray herald arrived on his last mission to the duke of Buckingham, and therefore, given the unusual reference to it in the Fastolf Relation, it may have been the only permanent barrier still serviceable in a much dilapidated defensive cordon.

Due to the absence of unbiased evidence from the Lancastrian side, a complete picture of how the king's army was positioned cannot be formed. However, according to the evidence, the following facts would have had little bearing on later Yorkist propaganda and therefore may have some foundation in truth.

1. The king and his household men had taken up position in St Peter's Street – that is, somewhere between the parish church and St Albans marketplace, at a location described as Goselowe or Sandeforthe. Before this, Henry was 'in the place of Edmond Westby, hunderder of the seid towne of Seint Albanus',[6] and no doubt was later moved so as to appear beside the king's standard, which that day was carried variously by Lord Sudeley, Steward of the Household, James Butler, Earl of Wiltshire, and Sir Philip Wentworth. Moreover, a statement in *Gregory's Chronicle* that 'Kyng Harry was in harnys hys owne propyr person'[7] gives credence to the theory that Henry was armed during the battle, wearing a harness (armour plate), and that he certainly was not just carrying a prayer book for protection.

2. Thomas Lord Clifford of Skipton (Yorkshire) was in command of the 'barreres of the same towne'[8] and defended these bravely, according to more than one account. The notice of Lord Clifford's valour was clearly not only a postscript to his death in battle, but also a tribute to his experience as a soldier, and therefore we may be sure that his command of the barricades at St Albans marketplace was a well-founded Yorkist observation.

3. The whereabouts of various other nobles prior to the battle of St Albans is not documented, and therefore we may suppose that before 'the larum

belle was ronge'[9] from the clock tower, warning of an imminent attack, most of these men were still with the king in St Peter's Street, awaiting orders. The duke of Buckingham may have been positioned near the barrier at St Peter's Church, along with 'Sir Richard Harrington, Bertin Entwistle and John Hanford knights, Breknok squire and John Swythman',[10] as the Fastolf Relation indicates that intermediaries were used on Mowbray herald's last mission to the town. However, in view of the sudden northerly advance of the duke of York and a surprise split in Yorkist forces, this area must at some point have been reinforced, and therefore must have caused a similar division in the king's army.

Topographically, the area that the Lancastrians had chosen to defend covered the triangular marketplace and the whole length of St Peter's Street, ending at the parish church of St Peter. However, it will be remembered that all along this route there was a jumble of largely unbroken houses and buildings which, according to sources, hindered movement when battle was joined and could not be breached by the Yorkists during their first assault. Therefore, apart from one or two inevitable gaps between the rows of houses that lined the eastern side of the marketplace and St Peter's Street, it is evident that the 2,000 men at Buckingham's disposal would not have been over-extended, and in fact could be considered as rather fortunate in their position.

No doubt the point at which the preliminary skirmishing ended and the real battle began was a confused affair and difficult to follow even by those involved in it, but the main attack by the Yorkists on the town barriers and the stout defence by the Lancastrians is reflected in the fact that York and the Nevilles could make no headway. According to the Stow Relation:

> [the king] hering of the seid dukis coming, commaunded his hooste to slee all maner [of] lordis, knightes, squierers, gentilmen and yomen that mighte be taken on the party of the forseid duc of Yorke. This done the forseid lorde Clifforde kepte so strongly the barreres of the same towne that the forseid duc of Yorke mighte in no wise with all the power that he hadde entre nor breke into the seid town.[11]

Apart from York's advance on the barrier near St Peter's Church, it is known that 'The Erle of warwyk with the march men and othir Entyrd

the othir Ende of the towne, and ffawgth agayne the kyngis partye'.[12]
As a result of this manoeuvre, most of fighting was concentrated at the
junction of Shropshire Lane and St Peter's Street, with the main action
being located near the Castle Inn, which was to feature predominantly
later in the battle. Another Neville contingent may have advanced
along Sopwell Lane and up Holywell Hill, in an effort to break into the
marketplace from there, but it is clear that Lord Clifford and the earl of
Northumberland frustrated these sustained Yorkist attacks, in a holding
action that seems to have lasted for the best part of an hour. Even with
an advantage in numbers, the barricaded streets of the town would not
have proved easy to assault. Borderers armed with the longbow, the most
formidable missile weapon of the day, would have had great difficulty
targeting defenders who were ensconced behind barriers and houses,
and the only choice left open to the Yorkists would have been to try
and break up the defences with hand weapons, whilst trying to stave off
enemy blows from above.

It is a significant fact of the battle that the king's men were not well
equipped with archers, due to the fact that no levies were present in
their ranks. It is also true that most of the defenders, and certainly their
men at arms, were not wearing a full complement of armour, the nature
of their wounds proving that neither helmets nor gauntlets were in place
during the street-fighting. However, the Yorkist attack might have been
permanently thwarted if it had not been for one enterprising soldier in
Warwick's ranks. Both the Stow and Phillipps Relations give an account
of who ordered the next attack, who commanded it and what part of
the defences it was intended to breach. The writers also describe why
the assault succeeded when the battle was clearly developing into a stalemate. The Stow Relation states that:

> Therle of Warrewik knowing therof [the Yorkist impasse] toke and gadererd
> his meyne togeder with hym and brake inne by the gardyne side into the seid
> towne betweene the Signe of the Keye and the Chequer in Halywell Strete.
> And anoone as they were withinne the seid towne they blewe up trumpettes
> and cryed with abigge voyse 'Awarwik Awarwik', that mervaile it was to here.
> And until that tyme the forseid duc of Yorke mighte never have entred into
> the towne. And thanne with stronge hande they brake up the barreres and
> mightily faughte.[13]

In the Phillipps Relation, there is no doubt which soldier led the assault and achieved the Yorkist breakthrough:

> And Sir Robert Ocle [Ogle] tok 600 men of the Marchis and tok the Market-place or ony man was war; than the larum belle was ronge, and every man yed to harneys, for at that tyme every man was out of ther array, and they joynid batayle anon; and it was done with inne di [half] houre.[14]

The great detail and time spent by the authors of the Stow and Phillipps Relations on expounding this action is proof of local eye-witness knowledge of the street battle that followed. When describing the covert action behind the houses lining the marketplace, both the above statements make the point that someone other than the duke of York was responsible for breaking the stalemate at the barriers. After the battle, the earl of Warwick was made captain of the Calais gar-rison, the only English standing army aboard, and the very mention of his name in conjunction with the turning point of the battle gives the impression that the younger Neville earl was the instigator of the assault. However, the generalship of Warwick throughout the Wars of the Roses was flawed on numerous occasions, especially at the sec-ond battle of St Albans in 1461, and therefore we must not give 'the kingmaker' full credit for making the breakthrough possible. We must also remember that the Stow Relation formed a major part of Yorkist propaganda after the event, and as such it is not surprising that that Ogle's attack, with 600 men of the Marches, was not recorded in this official Yorkist source. After the battle Sir Robert received no reward for his action at St Albans, and he was not raised to the peerage until the reign of Edward IV. Nevertheless, we can be sure that it was he who led the assault on the marketplace, after a gap between the houses (or, indeed, between the inns) was found. Ordering his troops to exploit this breach in the royalist defences turned the tide of the battle in the Yorkists' favour, a manoeuvre which Warwick probably knew about, but failed to recognise in any major way.

Davies' Chronicle also states that Ogle and his men 'brake doune vyolently howses and pales on the este side of the toune, and entred into seynt Petres street sleyng alle tho that wythestoode theym',[15] and the Dijon Relation makes it clear that:

they took and blockaded the marketplace of the said village and part of [Warwick's] people found themselves in the middle of it and in this manner began to fight the one party against the other [however] because the place was small few of the combatants could set to work there and matters reached such a great extremity that four of those who were of the king's bodyguard were killed by arrows in his presence.[16]

Packed full of local knowledge, the above accounts of the fight for the marketplace vividly described firstly the shock of Ogle's attack; secondly, the fact that the area became suddenly filled with masses of men; and, thirdly, that the king and his household troops were suddenly and precipitately drawn into the fighting. Obstacles, including market stalls, buildings and the very fact that both sides' troops were now hemmed in to the front and rear by barricades, would have heightened the confusion of the street-fighting considerably. Also, now that the king had ventured, or had been purposely moved, closer to the action, the situation suddenly became far more critical for the royalists. Why had the king been allowed to place himself in such a vulnerable position? Was the move intentional, so that the Yorkists could see the king's standard advertising the dire consequences of treason? Or were the Lancastrian commanders now in a desperate position and, throwing caution to the wind, decided to risk the king's safety in an effort to ensure their own survival? Much to the consternation of the royalists, the reaction to the king's arrival had the reverse effect on Sir Robert Ogle's mind-set, and, despite the apparent show of majesty in the marketplace, his Marchmen began indiscriminately to let loose flights of arrows into the crowd before them.

At this point in the battle, due to the fact that the king's men were now beset on two fronts, the barricades were of no further use and were quickly abandoned by the royalists. Both in the marketplace and also at the barriers near St Peter's Church, the tide of battle suddenly turned in favour of the Yorkists and, chiefly, the Nevilles. The fight now centred on the very heart of St Albans. With York's men swarming down the broad thoroughfare of St Peter's Street, it would only have been a matter of minutes before the marketplace was literally crammed with the bodies of some 5,000 fighting men. Abbot Whethamstede later recorded a convincing description of the slaughter which ensued when the barricades collapsed and more of the Neville contingents streamed into the town:

...they [the Yorkists] soon sounded the trumpet and rushed into the middle of St Peter's Street, breaking down the barriers until they had the king's
battle-line in front of them. They fought each other for a short space of time
so fiercely that here you would have seen one man lying with his brain struck
out, there another with his arm cut off, there a third with his throat cut, there
a fourth with his chest pierced, and the whole place beyond filled with the
corpses of the slain, on this side and that and everywhere in every direction. And so powerfully at the time was shield driven back by shield and
targe by targe, threatening sword by sword, foot by foot and weapon-point
by weapon-point that for a time the outcome was in doubt to which side
victory would yield, and the dice of fate was unclear enough.[17]

Whethamstede's report, supporting the theory that the town barricades were makeshift and not permanent fixtures, may well have been
prompted by what he actually saw in the streets immediately after the
battle had ended. As previously explained, his graphic descriptions of
wounds to the body, limbs and head tend to support the claims that most
of the king's men did not have time to don their armour or, indeed, strap
on their helmets before battle commenced.

According to *Davies' Chronicle*, the king and most of his household
were now present and fighting in St Peter's Street and the market area.
They were clearly disadvantaged by their lack of defensive equipment,
but it is highly likely that at first they made some impact in the confined space available to them. Evidently, King Henry took no part in
this hand-to-hand fighting, due to his apparent abhorrence of violence.
However, it is recorded in the Phillipps Relation that the king was
wearing his armour, and other commentators state that he was vehemently against the Yorkists and their petitions to remove the duke of
Somerset, to the point of wanting to kill them, 'every mother's son'.
Although we cannot be sure of the veracity of this remark, men like
Somerset and Buckingham clearly thought that any danger to the king's
person was minimal when weighed against what could occur if royal
eyes were averted. Given that Henry did not arrive in the marketplace
until after the defences were breached, it is probable that the royalist
nobles thought it imperative to reinforce their vulnerability with a more
substantial symbol of sovereignty. To this end, *Davies' Chronicle* states, the
king arrived from the direction of St Albans Abbey, and, although it is
clear that Henry did not lodge here prior to the battle, we can well

imagine that the king's entrance into the marketplace would have been masked by confusion, and after the event may have been impossible to relate with any certainty.

However, regardless of the danger and the direction of the king's approach, with his banner displayed Henry was at some point directed towards the worst of the fighting:

> ...and duke Edmond [Somerset] wythe hym, and the duk of Bokyngham, the erle of Northumbrelonde, and the lorde Clyfforde and the lorde Sudeley beryng the kynges baner [and] the kyng that stoode under his baner was hurte in the necke wythe an arowe.[18]

Another account has it that 'the king himself was struck by an arrow in the shoulder, but it penetrated only a little of the flesh'.[19] Several other sources support the claim that the king's injury was a notable occurrence and one that might have easily caused his death. However, Abbot Whethamstede makes no mention of Henry's wound, and this begs the question whether the injury occurred at all. The fact that it is mentioned by Yorkist sources, hence supporting the claims of a near catastrophe, helped their propaganda succeed against the duke of Somerset and his supporters in the later Parliamentary Pardon, and this may suggest that the wound was minimal. Clearly, a difference of an inch or so in the trajectory of the arrow's flight would have been disastrous to both sides, and to the kingdom as a whole. If Henry had been struck cleanly in the neck by an arrow, or even through his mail collar (standard), then the result would have certainly proved fatal and beyond any attempted battlefield surgery. Therefore, taking into account all the above sources, and indeed bearing in mind what occurred next, we may be sure that the king was only slightly injured in the fight and that his wound was caused either by a ricocheting arrow or, alternatively, by one that actually pierced the king's shoulder armour (pauldron), thus lessening the impact and therefore the force of penetration.

However, it is at this point in the battle that the clarity begins to blur in Yorkist propaganda. With the duke of York's men bearing down upon the marketplace from the northern end of St Peter's Street, and all exits barred from the east by Neville contingents, the next few minutes of the battle cannot be verified by any one source. As with all attempts at reconstruction, there are alternative scenarios, and the final phase of the battle of St Albans is no exception. Indeed, the killings that were perpetrated in full view of those who fought may have occurred in the heat and confusion of battle, by chance or, indeed, by design. In short, the end of the fighting can be taken two ways, due to a 'cover-up' that was later made official by parliament in favour of the Yorkist lords. Some sources are clear as to what occurred in the streets of St Albans as midday approached, while others, mainly Yorkist, prefer to note that casualties occurred on a much wider and more haphazard scale. The truth must lie hidden somewhere between the official Yorkist pardon and the views of those more unbiased chroniclers who may have had little to gain from perpetrating a falsehood.

With the wounded king standing forlornly beneath his banner, his faithful household men would have closed ranks around him, and many were killed trying to protect Henry from further injury. Lord Sudeley, the first of his household to bear his banner, was hit in the face by an arrow, we are told, and the duke of Buckingham shared a similar fate, while all around them was a writhing mass of pushing bodies, clash-ing weapons and cries for help. No doubt the king's banner was picked up after Sudeley's downfall, and this was probably recovered by either the earl of Wiltshire or Sir Philip Wentworth, who were both later held responsible for casting the banner down and fleeing from the scene. However, it is clear from casualty reports that the king's household men fought bravely for some minutes, until it was apparent that all was lost. Fighting for their lives under a canopy of steel and falling arrows, it was now only a matter of minutes before the unrelenting Yorkist soldiers butchered every royalist in sight, including the king of England. It was at this point that Henry's banner, the rallying point of all English armies, vanished from sight. According to *Gregory's Chronicle*:

> The Erle of Wyltschyre bare the kyngys baner that day in the batayle, for he was at that tyme namyd but Syr Jamys Urmon, and thys sayde Jamys sette the kyngys baner agayne an howse ende and fought manly with the helys, for he was a feryd of lesynge of beute, for he was namyd the fayryd knyght of thys londe.[20]

The earl of Wiltshire apparently cast off what armour he had, ran from the marketplace into the abbey and, disguising himself as a monk, made a lucky escape while the fighting still raged. Other men, including Sir

Philip Wentworth, also decided to flee the marketplace, but it is clear that towards the end of the battle many of the king's men were being beaten back, either running into houses or trying to extricate themselves from the thicket of stabbing weapons which were multiplying by the minute. Pushed both backwards and sideways across the street, there would have been no escape from the mêlée, apart from seeking cover in buildings or cutting a route through the Yorkists to the western end of the marketplace, where two roads were still open and unaffected by the fighting. Even the duke of Buckingham, who had now sustained three arrow wounds, most likely limped away at this point and fled to the abbey and the sanctuary it offered. It is no wonder that the king, now alone and unprotected, suffered another bout of insanity soon after the battle and never fully recovered from the trauma of his ordeal. Indeed, it is this event that may have been responsible for his well-known revulsion at the sight of blood, which stayed with him for the rest of his unhappy life.

According to the Dijon Relation, while confusion still ruled in the streets the duke of York 'gave orders that the king should be taken and drawn out of the throng and put in the abbey in safety and thus it was done'[21] However, a different story was related by John Whethamstede who, after bemoaning the 'softness' of the king's troops, goes on to state that,

> The king, however, seeing that his men were either turned in flight or dead on the field, and that he was standing under his standard without any protection, without hope or relief, on the suggestion of a few who said that he should flee from the face of the bow, and escape from the dangers of the arrows, which kept flying about his head more thickly than snowflakes, took himself off to the tiny dwelling of a tanner and there stayed with his men, until the Duke of York came and greeted him.[22]

If the king was rushed into a nearby house out of harm's way, what price the rest of the king's men still fighting in the street and faced with a gathering tide of Yorkist soldiers, all eager to capitalise on their victory? Evidently, Whethamstede's statement infers that York had nothing to do with the king's removal to safety, and it seems that he was now free to exact his revenge on his rival, the duke of Somerset, away from prying eyes. The largely unbiased Dijon Relation gives a full and graphic account of what occurred inside and outside the Castle Inn, located at the junction of Shropshire Lane with St Peter's Street.

> At last when they had fought for the space of three hours the king's party seeing themselves to have the worst of it broke on one wing and began to flee and the Duke of Somerset retreated within an inn to save himself and hid. Which things seen by those of the said Duke of York [they] incontinent beset the said house all about. And there the Duke of York gave orders that the king should be taken and drawn out of the throng and put in the abbey in safety and thus it was done. And in this abbey took refuge also with him the Duke of Buckingham who was very badly wounded by three arrows. And incontinent this done [they] began to fight Somerset and his men who were in this place within the inn and defended themselves valiantly. And in the end after the doors were broken down the Duke of Somerset seeing that he had no other remedy took council with his men about coming out and did so, as a result of which incontinent he and all his people were surrounded by the Duke of York's men. And after some were stricken down and the Duke of Somerset had killed four of them with his own hand, it is said, he was felled to the ground with an axe and incontinent being so wounded in several places that there he ended his life.[23]

According to *Davies' Chronicle,* it was said that the duke of Somerset had heard a 'fantastyk' prophecy that he would someday die under a castle, and as a result he had avoided going to Windsor, dreading that the prediction might come true, 'but at Seynt Albonys ther was an hostry hauyng the sygne of a castelle, and before that hostry he was slayne'.[24]

Clearly, the Dijon Relation makes much of this episode as the climax not only to the battle, but also to the feud between York and Somerset. Likewise, Somerset's death is also mentioned in the letter to the archbishop of Ravenna, underlining the fact that York's ultimate ambition was to kill his rival, with him being unceremoniously dragged out of the mêlée and formally beheaded for his crimes. Therefore, as far as foreign commentators were concerned, York had exacted personal revenge on his rival to the extent of removing the king from the battle so that this might be done more effectively. The duke of Somerset probably realised that if he was captured by the Yorkists there would be no mercy and thus made a fighting exit from the Castle Inn in the vain hope that Henry might be on hand to save him. Thus, 'with [Somerset's] death the battle ceased at once, and without loss of time, the duke of York went to kneel before the king and ask his pardon for himself and his followers, as they had not done this in order to inflict any hurt upon his majesty, but in order to have Somerset'.[25]

After the event, and in keeping with Yorkist propaganda, Somerset was attacked for his conduct in general. In *Gregory's Chronicle*, for example, the case against the duke was particularly slanderous in stating that the people felt that 'the Duke of Somerset was worthy to suffer that dethe by so moche that he brought Kyng Harry at Claryngdon be-syde Saulysbury and there he toke hys grete sekenys',[26] thereby implying that Somerset might have maltreated the king in some way or even have speeded up the onset of his illness. Unfortunately, much like the Stow and Phillipps Relations, *Gregory's Chronicle* fails to mention who was personally responsible for killing Somerset outside the Castle Inn, and the episode is glossed over impeccably by Yorkist sources, which prefer to list Somerset among the casualties of the battle, along with other nobles such as the earl of Northumberland and Lord Clifford. Essentially, Somerset's death was seen by foreign sources as the culmination of private feuding and by at least one English commentator as retribution for his crimes. That York purposely sought out the duke of Somerset, cornered him in the street and then killed him with his own hand is one way to resolve the problem. However, judging by the evidence, there may be another, more plausible scenario, and this is linked with the deaths of the earl of Northumberland and Lord Clifford.

It will be remembered that during the attack on the town Lord Clifford had commanded at the 'barres' with great courage. This incident is enlarged upon by a chronicler who knew the Clifford family well, having been in the service of the earl of Northumberland in the days of his father, Henry Percy (nicknamed 'Hotspur'), who died at the battle of Shrewsbury in 1405. John Hardyng had been a soldier at the aforesaid battle and in later life wrote a *History of Britain* in the reign of Edward IV. Although his writing is clearly biased in favour of the Yorkists, he left this interesting description of the battle of St Albans, which poses a whole host of questions regarding the deaths of Somerset and of those nobles whom the Nevilles saw as their enemies:

Thei [the Yorkists] were put by from all their good entent,
And strauge were hold after many a daye,

To the thirty yere and thre by hole consent,
At sainct Albones then upon the Thursdaye,
Accompted then next afore Witsondaye,
Thei slewe the duke Edmond [then]of Somerset,
For cause he had the realms wele so lette.

Therle [then] of Northumberland was there,
Of sodein chaunce drawen furth with the kyng,
And slain unknowne by any manne ther were;
The lord Clifford, ouer busie in werkyng,
At the barres theim mette sore fighting,
Was slain that daye upon his owne assaut,
Aseche manne saied it was his owne defaute.

Therle of Wiltshire with five hundred menne,
Fled fro the kyng full fast that tyme a waye,
The duke of Buckyngham was hurte there then.
The kyng thei tooke and saved in good araye.[27]

Thomas Gascoigne's pro-Yorkist remark that the duke of Somerset was slain and that several other of the duke's supporters, such as Northumberland and Lord Clifford, were killed unintentionally also adds weight to Hardyng's interpretation. However, ranged against this evidence we must also consider that it was the Nevilles who posed an overriding threat to Yorkist strategy, and remember that it was they who had instigated the battle in the first place. John Hardyng implies that Clifford fell at the barricades leading an ill-advised assault, that Northumberland was slain by an unknown hand, and that the duke of Somerset was 'justifiably' killed by the Yorkists because he had mismanaged the kingdom. In this apology, therefore, Hardyng was clearly aiming to please the current regime and particularly to satisfy Edward IV, in an effort to raise all England, and particularly the north, against Edward's mortal enemies, the Scots. Therefore elements of partiality were undoubtedly included in Hardyng's work. The earl of Northumberland, for example, was clearly not with the king by 'sodein chaunce' in May 1455, and equally he was not a bystander during the street-fighting that occurred at St Albans. Similarly, Lord Clifford is portrayed in Hardyng's account as causing his own death by leading a suicidal assault on the Yorkist position. It is highly likely that Hardyng fabricated his account of St Albans in favour of the Yorkist court, to the extent of leaving out the fact that Somerset, Northumberland and Clifford were not killed by accident, but by design.

This alternative viewpoint is hidden deep within Yorkist propaganda and concealed not by what was put into reports after St Albans, but by what was left out. Did the duke of York give explicit orders that King Henry should be removed from danger so that he might freely kill Somerset, or was it that the duke was already dead, along with Northumberland and Clifford, long before York arrived in the market-place? Faced with this choice, we may either point an accusing finger at York and the Nevilles and conclude that both parties had everything to gain from the deaths of their opposite numbers, or alternatively suggest that in the heat of battle the king was taken out of the throng with the express purpose of assassinating a select group of nobles. There is no doubt that troops raised by the Neville earls featured predominantly in York's army and that Abbot Whethamstede made much of their role in his account, even to the extent of blaming them for the widespread looting that occurred in his town after the battle. Similarly, among the royalist dead were men from families associated with the earl of Northumberland, such as Sir John Stapleton, Avery Mauleverer, Ralph Babthorpe and William Curwen, not to mention Lord Clifford – a statement of fact which certainly suggests that some Percy retainers were killed intentionally. Therefore, did the duke of York have no control whatsoever over the Nevilles? This seems to have been the case at the beginning of the battle, and following the main assault on the barricades York may have totally lost contact with them in an effort to rescue King Henry from the mêlée. In fact, if this is what occurred then we may absolve York from any direct blame attached to the 'execution' of Somerset, since he may not even have been present in the market-place at the time of his death.

According to the Dijon Relation, Somerset was killed by 'the Duke of York's men'[28] after York had ordered the removal of Henry from the fighting. Could it be that York returned to the marketplace after removing the king, to find Somerset, Northumberland and Clifford already butchered in the street? And if so, did he find his Neville relatives proudly standing over their bodies, waiting to be congratulated by the leading and most influential member of their family?

Either way, the deed had been done and in Lancastrian eyes it would be later regarded as cold-blooded murder. In the last throes of royal resistance, three leading members of the English nobility had been brutally slain and several others, including Somerset's son, had been badly injured. According to the Stow Relation:

> And at the same batelle of lordes of name were hurte: the king our souveraigne lorde in the nekke with an arow, the duc of Bokingham and the lorde Sudeley in the visages with an arow, therle of Stafforde in the righte hande with an arow, therle of Dorsett [Somerset's son] sore hurte that he mighte not goo but that he was caried home in a carte, and Sir John Wenlok knighte in like wise hurte and caried in achare and divers other knightes and squieres soore hurte. And the substaunce of the kinges hooste [were] despoiled of here harneis [armour] at theire owne requeste and delivery made to the dukes hooste for salvacion of theire lyves. And therle of Wiltshire and Thorpe with many other fledde and caste awaye thaire harneis in diches and wodes.[29]

Awash with blood, spent arrows and broken weapons, the streets of St Albans were now in utter confusion. The body count would be numbered in tens rather than hundreds, but if one moment can be judged as the start of the Wars of the Roses then this was indisputably that moment. The blood feud and the shadow it would cast across successive generations had been instigated by ambitious men who had used the politics of others in order to satisfy their own needs. To begin with, Neville troops had not thought twice about skirmishing with the enemy right under the nose of their commander-in-chief; they had been oblivious to the fact that once the battle was underway they might have killed their king with a random arrow; they had stood by while a portion of the nobility was first targeted and then unchivalrously hacked to death, without being offered ransom; and, much like armies on foreign soil, they were now about to loot and ravage an English town in repayment for their ordeal. If the aim of the duke of York had been to arrest his rival Somerset, or indeed to execute him for his crimes against Henry and the kingdom, it was certainly not his intention to kill or anger any other members of the nobility. Alienation was the last thing that York hoped to achieve at St Albans, and thus he had, according to Buckingham's intuition, adopted a restrained attitude, entered into negotiations and tried to keep his men at a safe distance. However, Buckingham had not bargained on how the

Nevilles might react to these delaying tactics. In fact, the Nevilles clearly had another agenda, due to their feud with the Percys in the north, not to mention with Somerset in Wales. York's sudden advance was primarily instigated by his predatory Neville allies, whom he had failed to control. His aim of securing the king and then, if need be, using force to arrest Somerset was therefore thwarted by his own allies' violent desire to kill their indigenous enemies.

With the king's men in complete rout, or being precariously guarded by their captors, the focus now turned from St Albans marketplace to the abbey, where it was said that the duke of Buckingham and the earl of Wiltshire had taken refuge. Since the king had also been rushed there in the heat of battle and some of York's men were reported in the vicinity soon after the rout had occurred, it was now imperative that the Yorkists follow up their victory with Henry's capture. The Dijon Relation takes up the story and reveals that when he finally had chance to speak to Henry face to face, York, despite his rebellious actions, behaved like a loyal subject and certainly did not in any way undermine the king's authority:

> The battle lasted until two and a half hours after noon and this done the Duke of York's men took themselves to the abbey to kill the Duke of Buckingham and the treasurer, who is called the Earl of Wiltshire, who had retreated there with the king, but the said Duke of York would not suffer it but sent his herald to the king to inform him that he must choose which he preferred, either to hand over the two lords as prisoners into his hands, or that they should be killed in front of him and to put himself in danger once more. Wherefore the king agreed freely to allow him to arrest the said two lords and so he did, in particular the Duke of Buckingham. And when all these things were done the Duke of York entered within the abbey and went before the king's person and there went on his knees to him crying mercy for whatever way he might have offended and for the peril in which he had put his person and many other good and humble words, showing him that he had not gone against him but against the traitors to his crown, and in the end before the Duke of York went away from there the king pardoned him everything and took him in his good grace.[30]

The actual fighting at St Albans had lasted from about 10 a.m. to around midday, but the rout and the point at which the king proclaimed 'that all manner of people shulde cease of theire malice'[31] may have prolonged the battle to well into the afternoon. To corroborate this, the precise evidence contained in the Dijon Relation states that the battle lasted until 2.30 pm. Some attention must therefore be given to the duration of the fighting, and we may be sure that the battle did not last half an hour, as some historians have claimed. Instead, it can be judged to have included at least an hour of skirmishing, followed by a stand-off at the barricades and thereafter an intense bout of street-fighting, in which several events and manoeuvres occurred. The rout, as always, is difficult to calculate regarding time, but the Dijon Relation is remarkably precise (and does not use Roman numerals to complicate matters) when describing the cycle of events. Indeed, all the relevant sources make it abundantly clear that the battle of St Albans was certainly not deserving of the label of a 'non-battle'. Most accounts, except that of C.A.J. Armstrong, are wildly off the mark and, due to the low casualty rate sustained during the battle, the duration of the fighting has received short shrift from many writers. It is interesting to speculate what might have occurred if contingents supplied by the duke of Norfolk, the earl of Shrewsbury, Lord Cromwell and Sir Thomas Stanley had arrived in time to participate in the fighting. That they did not take part in the battle, and that some stood idly by on the sidelines awaiting the result, speaks volumes about the perceived seriousness of York's bid to seize his rival. St Albans was therefore seen by contemporaries as a major 'journey' (battle), not only because of the long-term effects of the Wars of the Roses, but also because of the way it hindered a peaceable settlement. It was not the beginning of civil war, but the battle of St Albans certainly succeeded admirably in inspiring revenge in the minds of all those sons who had lost their fathers in the fighting. Additionally, we may speculate that the battle placed a degree of guiltiness in the hearts of all York's men, especially those who had re-defined the codes of chivalry in a frenzied bout of cold-blooded murder.

7

The Fate of the Kingdom

According to the historian William Stubbs, 'the first battle of St Albans sealed the fate of the kingdom',[1] and certainly, with regard to factionalism and the way this polarised the English nobility thereafter, medieval England would never be the same again. Contemporaries did not ignore the seriousness of the encounter, and, although the battle was censored by the Yorkists immediately afterwards, it was seen by many as a national disaster – an episode that would have undoubtedly been more catastrophic had King Henry been killed in the fighting. As for casualties, most chroniclers did not exaggerate their figures, as was the standard practice of the day, and some authors may even have suppressed the real death toll, certainly regarding lesser ranks, to accord with Yorkist propaganda. Alternatively, a tendency towards lower casualty figures may indicate that certain individuals were sought out and targeted at St Albans, instead of being randomly slaughtered. The significance of the battle should not therefore be underestimated, and the way in which the victors attempted to cover up the truth in official documents after the event betrays the seriousness of their actions.

Omitting sixteenth-century historians, the highest casualty estimate for the battle is that given in the Phillips Relation, which states that 400 men died in the battle, 'and as many or mo hurt',[2] while the lowest estimate is given in the *London Chronicle*, which names three lords and a single knight plus 'xxv squyers with other people'.[3] However, in the majority of sources there is a consensus of opinion that the death toll was relatively slight. As a supplement to the above rather haphazard accounting, the Stow Relation provides a much more detailed record of the casualties:

> At whiche fighte were slayne of lordis of name the forseid lorde Clifforde, the duc of Somersett and therle of Northumbreland, Sir Barton Entewsell knighte, William Zowche, John Botreaux, Rafe Babthorpe and his sone, William Corvin, William Coton, receyvor of the duchere of Lancaster, Gilbert Faldinger, Reynold Griffyn, John Dawes, Elys Woode, John Eythe, Robert Wodewarde, Gilbert Skarlok and Raufe Willoughby squieres, a gentilman of courte, Roger Mercrofte the queens messenger, Hawkin the kinges porter, Maleners, Padington and William Boteler yomen and xxv mo whos names be nat knowen and of hem that bene slayne bene buried at Seint Albanus xlviii [48] personnes.[4]

A similar casualty list is included in the Phillipps Relation, along with a detailed report of the injured, which echoes the above in all but a few instances. Evidently, some of the named individuals in both accounts actually survived the battle but unfortunately neither source gives an indication of how many men were killed on each side – an all-important factor with regard to determining how ferocious the fighting became and how closely the rout was followed. In the Dijon Relation it is stated that 200 'or thereabouts'[5] were slain at the battle, while *Davies' Chronicle* put the casualty figure at 'lx [60] persones of gentilmen and of other'.[6] A continuation of the *Polychronicon* attests to 140 men killed, while a Paston letter sent by John Crane suggests a figure in the region of 'vi score [120]'.[7] In addition to the above figures, we should also balance this evidence against a casualty report from the Register of the Archdeacons of St Albans, which lists the names of over forty casualties, all of whom were buried in the abbey and in St Peter's churchyard. However, even when dealing with proportionately lower estimates the sources vary considerably, and therefore we may never know the true death toll. We can hazard a guess that about 100 men died at St Albans, taking into account the casualties in the rout and those sustained by the lower classes of soldier, about whom little or no evidence exists.

As previously stated, contemporaries recorded that a number of royalist soldiers sustained arrow wounds during the battle, and this fact alone may have contributed to a higher casualty rate – not to mention the possibility that some of these individuals suffered from diseased wounds long after the event. It is known that injuries inflicted by either barbed or bodkin arrowheads, along with the dirt and fragments of metal and cloth they introduced to the body and bloodstream, were the wounds feared more than any other. Indeed, even if some men arrived home safely carrying these injuries and were treated by local physicians, this probably did not ensure their survival. Therefore the after-effects of the battle may have filled many a local churchyard with gentry and commoners alike. For example, Bertin Entwistle, the veteran soldier from Lancashire, was listed among the St Albans dead, but according to sources he did not die of his wounds until some days after the battle. Finally interred in St Peter's Church on 28 May, his epitaph was recorded by John Weever more than 150 years later:

> Here lyeth Syr Bertin Entwisel knt, who was born in Lancaster Shyre, and was vicound and Bailiff of Constantin who died the xxviii of May on whose soul Jesu have mercy.[8]

John Leland, the Tudor antiquary, located Entwistle's memorial under the place of the lectorium of the quire, but unfortunately nothing now remains of his last resting place apart from rubbings from sections of his armorial brass (the centre of the body and the left leg), still in the possession of the Society of Antiquaries. Also buried in St Peter's Church were Ralph Babthorpe and his son, both mentioned in the above casualty lists, and also Thomas Pakington, the sword-bearer of the earl of Northumberland, who doubtless had been cut down along with his master in the marketplace. It is not known how many other soldiers were buried in St Peter's, but Weever's statement recording significant burials there has most likely been confused with the larger casualties inflicted at the second battle of St Albans in 1461, when much greater armies were engaged.

All of the leading nobles killed during the battle received burial in the abbey church when it was safe to do so, and it is said that these bodies were unearthed below the altar of the Lady Chapel, where they had been seen 'in their rusty armour'[9] by workers undertaking floor renovations in the late nineteenth century. Whether these skeletons in armour were actually the remains of Somerset, Northumberland and Clifford is, of course, highly conjectural, and, since the excavation was not properly recorded at the time, the evidence for their burials cannot be verified. However, according to E.B. de Fonblanque, the renowned Percy annalist, the earl of Northumberland was at some point exhumed from St Albans and reburied in York Minster, where a window showing him along with his wife and children was still extant in 1590. It was either here, or in the Percy church of St Denys, also in York, that Northumberland's body was finally interred – neither the first nor the last of his family to be butchered in the Wars of the Roses. As for Somerset and Clifford, the *Paston Letters* record that all three nobles were first buried at St Albans, and, since a memorial to Lord Clifford once existed in the Lady Chapel, it is possible that at least two out of the three royalist nobles are still interred somewhere in the abbey.

Among the injured royalists who managed to escape the field was Henry Fylongley, whom the Phillipps Relation noted for his bravery during the battle. Fylongley was a servant of Sir John Fastolf and had been repeatedly 'shet thorwe the armys in iii. or iiii. placys'[10] – which again attests to the fact that, at least at the onset of the battle for the marketplace, a hail of arrows had been indiscriminately unleashed on the royalist troops, with the hope of causing the maximum amount of confusion and panic. In a letter written by William Barker to William Worcester in June 1455, Fylongley was said to be still recovering at his home, tended by his wife, and it was feared that his injuries would keep him incapacitated for some time, much to the consternation of his friends. It is not known whether he fully recovered, but many like him did not. An analysis of the casualty lists reveals that the main cause of injuries and deaths at St Albans was the fact that Yorkist archers shot at the royalist troops while they were massed in such a confined area. Many of Henry's household men were among the dead, and this attests to the highly dangerous situation that developed around the king's standard when Sir Robert Ogle's men first targeted them with their powerful bows. Others of the king's household, afterwards called cowards, managed to escape the street-fighting long before Somerset, Northumberland and Clifford met their deaths, which again testifies to the panic and confusion that resulted from Ogle's attack. For example, the Stow Relation states that the earl of Wiltshire, Thorpe and many others fled the marketplace, casting away their armour in ditches and woods to speed their escape. The king's standard was thrown down in the rush to evacuate the area, because royalist troops had no way of replying to the weight of missiles falling on their exposed position. Add to this the original surprise of Ogle's breakthough into the town, and it is clear that those royalists who fled the fighting were not faint-hearted but were responding to an extremely alarming situation which could neither be counteracted nor sustained with the weapons available to them.

Notably, the Register of the Archdeacons of St Albans recorded that most of the casualties were located to the north, in St Peter's ward, which then extended south from the parish church to a point bisecting the marketplace. This area obviously included the whole length of St Peter's Street, the area around the Castle Inn, the junction of Shropshire Lane and a portion of the shambles, which not only confirms contemporary accounts of the fighting, but also suggests that it was here that most of the royalist force was located and shot at by Ogle's archers. Interestingly, the parish boundary can still be seen marked on a wooden lintel between the houses lining the east side of what is now Chequer Street.

The deaths of leading nobles and members of the king's household; the indiscriminate pillage of the town by Yorkist troops and the capture of King Henry by a faction of the nobility whose aim had been to rid the country of a corrupt regime were events that had to be condoned by the victors. However, it is clear that the Nevilles had complicated the issue by also killing their local enemies – a calamity that was evidently not foreseen before the fighting began. How was this 'murder' to be condoned by the duke of York? With the king in a position to be manipulated once more, could York both console the injured Henry and also accord with those royalists who had been, in Yorkist eyes, caught on the wrong side? How would the Yorkists deal with the families of Somerset, Northumberland and Clifford, all of whom had sons waiting in the wings to avenge their father's deaths? Judging by the way the

Yorkists changed their story after reaching London, it seems that their propaganda evolved out of many attempts at fabrication. The resulting Parliamentary Pardon would merely postpone the inevitable blood feud and dynastic civil war, which surfaced in 1459, and the fact that both sides remained irreconcilable in the interim would continue to plague King Henry who, in his own indomitable way, sought and tried to effect a peaceful settlement.

As stated earlier, St Albans was not the first battle of a dynastic civil war, but it was the beginning of the tensions that would instigate it. York had made his peace with the king in the sanctity of St Albans Abbey, and it was much to Henry's credit that order was restored in the town thereafter. Thus far, York had exorcised the gut-wrenching humiliation of Dartford, but at a high price. Many contemporaries would have understood his quarrel with the 'scheming' duke of Somerset and the reason behind Somerset's apparent execution, but who, apart from the Nevilles, would be willing to condone the assassinations of Northumberland and Clifford and the deaths of many of the king's household men?

After spending the remainder of Thursday 22 May in his apartments within the abbey, Henry was conducted to Westminster, where he arrived at 6 p.m. the following day. With York riding on the king's right and Salisbury on his left, accompanied by Warwick ahead, bearing the sword of state, appearances were boldly maintained in a general procession that same evening. It was important that Henry should not appear to the populace as a Yorkist prisoner, even though the king may have privately thought differently about the whole affair. However, the tension between York and the king reached a new climax at St Paul's on Whitsunday, when Henry insisted that the duke, not the archbishop, should place the crown on his head – a clear reminder of his sanctity to all who stood witness. Indeed, from this point on the king appears to have distanced himself from his keepers, and after writs were sent out on 26 May to summon parliament, he immediately vacated the bishop of London's palace and travelled first to Windsor and then to Hertford, in an effort to shut out the traumatic events which had suddenly befallen him.

Soon after this, Henry seems to have required at least two weeks of medical treatment and, although he was seen to function normally during the next parliament, the threat of another bout of deep depression placed a tremendous strain on Yorkist security. In the end, Henry's continued instability and his inability to retain the mantle of kingship would bring about renewed factionalism, the emergence of Queen Margaret as a political leader, and a renewal of hostilities. However, with regard to the battle of St Albans, *Gregory's Chronicle* maintained that 'the kynge lete alle thys mater be in a dormon a grete and a long tyme aftyr... for hyte was noo seson to trete of pesse, for sum were welle cotente and sum evylle plesyd'[11] with York's action. This uneasy peace was also noted in a letter written from Bruges to the archbishop of Ravenna on 3 June 1455, in which the gravity of Henry's melancholy was so pronounced that the writer proclaimed that 'the king has forbidden anyone to speak about it [the battle] on pain of death'.[12] No doubt all this uncertainty, along with the need to re-establish Yorkist respectability, made the first phase of Yorkist propaganda more difficult to initiate.

Prior to holding parliament, it was imperative that York grasped firm control of the government which had so recently been taken away from him. The duke took for himself the privileged office of constable of England; Archbishop Bourchier was requested to retain the Great Seal; and the treasury was given to his brother, Viscount Bourchier. Salisbury and Warwick were already joint wardens of the West March towards Scotland, but now this appointment was confirmed to them for the next twenty years – a situation which, in conjunction with the appointment of Warwick as captain of Calais, confirms Neville pre-eminence at the battle of St Albans, which was, after all, won primarily by their men. In fact, the favouring of the houses of Neville and Bourchier is the most striking aspect of Yorkist munificence. Precious few rewards were given to either nobles or gentry for their military service at St Albans, apart from six named individuals, and the need for restraint was further dictated by the likelihood of an act of resumption in the forthcoming parliament. In short, York's hands were tied by his own need to restore 'normal' political life. His need for former royalists, some of whom had been badly injured in the battle, to 'come inne... and draw the lyne'[13] with him, and with those of his party who had opposed them across the barricades, was to be a constant feature in his forthcoming propaganda. With this in mind, the duke of Buckingham, Sir John Wenlock, and even the earl of Dorset, Somerset's son, were to be 'forgiven' for their part in the battle, along with those ambivalent peers who had stood idly by on the sidelines awaiting a result. To avoid political isolation, York had to balance his actions with his desire to retain loyal support, and although the Nevilles and Bourchiers must have felt well satisfied with their scoop of vacant offices and titles, men such as Lord Clinton, Lord Cobham and Sir Robert Ogle paid the price of York's restrictions.

All now awaited the calling of parliament, which assembled as planned on 9 July 1455, giving the Yorkists ample time to prepare speeches favourable to themselves and detrimental to the duke of Somerset and his followers. Attendance at Westminster was average, but conspicuous by their absence were the duke of Exeter and Henry Beaufort, the new duke of Somerset (the latter had been in Warwick's close custody since the Yorkists had returned to London). By all accounts, Somerset's young heir was unappeasable – and was doubtless more offended when he heard that the opening sermon of parliament blamed the battle of St Albans wholly on his father and two of his followers, Thomas Thorpe and William Joseph. It was stated that these three had misled the king into thinking that York, Warwick and Salisbury had gathered their forces with rebellious intent. The first part of King Henry's speech, probably delivered by Archbishop Bourchier, then described how Somerset had used the king's power to further his feud with York. Next, the two letters written by the Yorkists prior to the battle were read out and the archbishop assured the commons that York, Warwick and Salisbury had come to the king at St Albans as loyal vassals and had taken great pains to clarify their honourable intentions before battle commenced.

Jean-Philippe Genet is one of the few historians to have analysed sections of the parliamentary speeches, and in his opinion the two letters sent to the king prior to the battle of St Albans had not been altered or concocted for the sake of the speech. Genet pointed out that the tone of the letters was one of extreme piety and loyalty and that they were included in parliament as concrete proof that rebellion had never been York's intent.[14] Apart from this, many at Westminster that day, including the king, would have immediately noticed any Yorkist fabrication if the letters had been in changed in any biased way. Henry's speech went on to state that he was in no doubt of the Yorkists' loyalty and that if he had seen the letters prior to the battle, which he said he had not, he would have trusted their contents and acted upon them. Thus, through casting Somerset as the traitor and the king as misinformed, the battle of St Albans became a loyal action and not a Yorkist insurgency. The closing declaration of the pardon decreed:

We therefore considering the premises, declare... our said cousins and all those persons who came with them in their fellowship to the said town of St Albans, the said 22nd day, and all other persons who... helped them, our true and faithful liegemen... And that none of our said cousins, the Duke of York, and the Earls of Warwick and Salisbury, nor any of the said persons coming or being with them, nor any of their... helpers... be impeached, sued, vexed, grieved, hurt or molested in any wise in their bodies, lands, or goods, for any thing supposed or claimed to have been done to or against our persons, crown, or dignity.[15]

There then followed an oath of allegiance to the king and a ritual signing of the document by those present, in this case thirty-three lords temporal and twenty-seven lords spiritual. In effect, by putting pressure on the king to accept their prepared speeches, which promised the hope of peace and unity, the Yorkists had pandered to the king's dearest wishes. Henry, by agreeing, had once again fallen foul of corrupt councillors – this time York and the Nevilles. He had proved to be as malleable as ever, even with regard to his memory of events immediately prior to the battle, and he had also willingly agreed to the 'lawful' killings of three of his highest-ranking nobles. The parliamentary proceedings closed on 31 July, with the declaration of a general pardon for all offences committed before 8 July, the earliest recipients being Lord Egremont and his brother on 6 August and the infamous duke of Exeter a few days later. York's need to heal the wounds of St Albans was great indeed, and for the present he had succeeded in concealing the transgressions of his allies.

The Parliamentary Pardon stifled the fierce recriminations that might have surfaced after the battle, but the bill had clearly not been without its problems in the making. In the Phillipps Relation, written soon after the battle and well before parliament sat on 9 July, responsibility for the battle was placed squarely on the shoulders of Lord Clifford, Ralph Percy (a younger son of the earl of Northumberland), Thomas Thorpe, Thomas Tresham and William Joseph. This blacklist was eventually changed in parliament to add Somerset in place of Clifford and to remove the names of those whom York wished to placate. Tresham and Joseph, it may be supposed, had fled like Thorpe from St Albans and were therefore easy targets to include next to those who had been killed. However, it was also important for the Yorkists not to blame the battle on powerful men, and thus the final list of traitors was not finalised until it had been decided that individuals such as the new earl of Northumberland (then Lord Poynings) and John Lord Clifford had been reconciled with York.

Another incident which probably hastened the need for the naming of scapegoats was the action of Lord Cromwell, who had not been at St Albans, but who nonetheless seemed paranoid about how he might be implicated in the Yorkist indictments. While parliament was in session on 17 July, Cromwell suddenly, without notice, excused himself to the king 'of all the steryng or moevyng of the male journey of Seynt Albones', and on hearing of this Warwick hastened to court, swearing that Cromwell was a liar and that he was the 'begynner of all that journey'.[16] Cromwell was so much alarmed by Warwick's revealing outburst that he immediately begged the earl of Shrewsbury to come to Charing Cross for his protection. Proclamations against bearing arms were issued, but thereafter the Yorkists travelled daily to Westminster, armed to the teeth, their barges stuffed with weapons and men at arms. It was the shape of things to come, and even though the incident between Warwick and Cromwell was isolated and more to do with the apportioning of property rights than of blame for the battle, the Parliamentary Pardon was no safeguard for a bill about which it was said that only a few days afterwards, 'mony a man groged full sore nowe it is passed'.[17]

Evidently, the Yorkist lords compiled their speeches with a view to limiting damage, but their words only postponed the factionalism that was later to cause so much unrest. With men like Archbishop Bourchier and, later, Sir John Wenlock as Yorkist speakers, their propaganda may have sounded wholly convincing to both Lords and Commons and may have seemed acceptable to many who wished to avoid further strife. However, the fact that Somerset had been punished for his crimes changed nothing with regard to who ruled England. Parliament was not always in session and soon it was clear that the king was, yet again, incapable of ruling the country. The bill which decided that York would have to be appointed protector for a second term of office was witnessed by the king at Westminster on 19 November 1455.

> We, considering the petition of the commons and the infirmity with which it has pleased the Most High Saviour to visit our person, an affliction which hinders us from the actual execution of the protection and defence of the realm and of the church of England, and considering that if we are troubled with numerous matters of business, the speed of our recovery will be

impaired, and reposing full confidence in the circumspection and industry of our most dear cousin Richard Duke of York. By the advice and assent of the lords spiritual and temporal and the assent of the commons of our realm of England, assembled in our present parliament, ordain and constitute our cousin to be protector and defender and our principal councillor of our realm of England and of the church of England.[18]

Renewing his allegiance to an essentially vacant throne, York once again assumed the mantle of authority. How patient he was, and how his desire for the throne must have been increased by Henry's frailty and inability to rule the kingdom. With a renewed feud in the West Country in full swing, between Lord Bonville and the earl of Devon, and a battle at Clyst boding more unrest between the two sides, the Yorkists yet again established themselves in government, and succeeded where the king had failed. However, as in the past, York's protectorship was not to last long, and in February 1456, with the king in better health, York was formally discharged from his duties. The unrelenting cycle of fortune and adversity left the Yorkist lords once more out in the cold and vulnerable to attack.

Later that year, the queen removed her husband from the unfriendly atmosphere in London to the Midlands, where the court remained and ruled England for the next four years. At a council meeting at Coventry on 16 October, the king's household, led now by Margaret, staged a coup. The chancellor and the Privy Seal were dismissed, leaving York and the Nevilles even more isolated. Then, on 5 November, the dukes of Exeter and Somerset, aided by the earl of Shrewsbury, attempted to ambush the earl of Warwick on his way to London. An attack on the duke of York followed soon after, this time at Coventry, and by the following year it seemed that the Yorkists were in mortal danger. Had it not been for King Henry, it is highly likely that at some point York and his allies would have been singled out and assassinated, in the name of those who had lost fathers in the streets of St Albans. However, it appeared that the king believed it was still possible to produce a negotiated settlement between the various parties, and to this end he arranged a council meeting for 27 January 1458, with a view to addressing matters as yet unresolved.

However, nothing was resolved at the so-called 'Love Day' of 16 March, which was a complete fiasco, arranged by a king who had once again overlooked issues of much deeper significance. With hundreds of armed retainers in London and men like Lord Egremont and the duke of Exeter loose in the city, it was no surprise that this event did little to alleviate private tensions and the desire for vengeance. In fact, the assembly of lords and the pretence of harmony precipitated the onset of more violence. In the council chamber, the terms of arbitration were firstly that the Yorkists would pay a cash recompense to the families who had suffered by their hands at St Albans, and secondly that a perpetual memorial for the slain would be built in the abbey church – also at the Yorkists' cost. In theory, York was to pay out some 5,000 marks in compensation, but this was made out in tallies yet to be issued. A deal was also struck whereby York could export wool to pay for his share of the endowment, terms that were hardly a penance for his part in the 'murder' of Somerset, Northumberland and Clifford. Potentially far more costly was the promise to settle land in lieu of compensation, but yet again the terms of honouring such an agreement would soon be overtaken by events. Guilty as charged, York and the Nevilles paid the first instalment of their blood money in 1459. Henry characteristically misjudged the situation, and a distinct reversal of fortunes followed later the same year, when a council at Coventry dictated that the Yorkists should be indicted of treason for causing 'the execrabill and moost detestible dede by them doon at Seint Albones'.[19]

Significantly, the two contending factions that met in the ensuing bout of civil war had already seen their families' blood shed at St Albans. The Yorkist transgression had been resurrected in public for all to see, and now it was the Nevilles' turn to pay for the deaths of Somerset, Northumberland and Clifford. Worse still, a new and more dangerous enemy had been made in Margaret, Henry's queen, and, with the sons of those who had been killed at St Albans crying out for blood, it was soon clear that Margaret's intentions were built on a much stronger foundation than her pious husband. In fact, her aim was to destroy York and all his party, no matter what additional damage this might inflict on her adopted country.

The battle of Blore Heath and the disastrous encounter at Ludford caused the Yorkist lords to flee the country in 1459. After the battle of Northampton in 1460, York would try to appropriate the crown for himself. However, his desire to be accepted as Henry's chief council-lor and perfect champion was an ambition that he was never to realise and, on a bitter cold December day in 1460, he was tricked, surrounded and butchered by a Lancastrian army under the command of a new

Somerset, Northumberland and Clifford. The battle of Wakefield also sealed the fate of many of the duke of York's principal adherents, including his son, the earl of Rutland (killed by John Lord Clifford in the rout), and the earl of Salisbury, who was executed at Pontefract Castle after being captured. It was left to the earl of Warwick and York's son Edward to pursue their fathers' killers. The result of this further bloodletting would eventually prove fatal to the Percys, the Cliffords and the Beauforts; in fact, it was to extinguish the male line of the Beauforts and seriously injure the fortunes and lives of the Percys and the Cliffords as the civil wars progressed.

Crucially, the first battle of St Albans marked the continuation of one feud and the beginning of another, far greater problem for English kings. Before Thursday 22 May 1455, feuding English families and localised rebellion had been mostly controlled. After the battle, political life would never be the same again. However, it is a mistake to think that the first battle of St Albans produced an immediate slide into anarchy and a long 'winter of discontent';[20] in fact, the encounter had far more dangerous and long-lasting consequences. With regard to the way the Wars of the Roses were fought from then on, it caused a greater willingness to resort to violent action rather than mediation on the battlefield. It prevented successful arbitration between the two contending sides of York and Lancaster for at least thirty-five years. It brought to an end the traditional chivalric practice of ransoming prisoners and, worse, the dynastic struggle it initiated caused a genuine fear in succeeding generations that the same thing could happen all over again.

Maps and
Genealogical Table

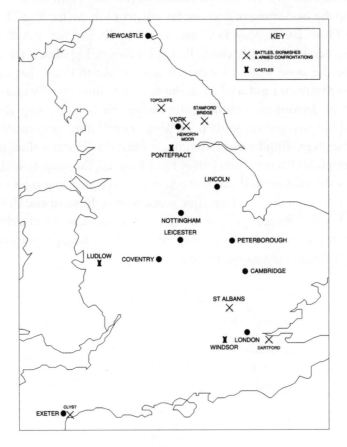

1 England 1452–1455.

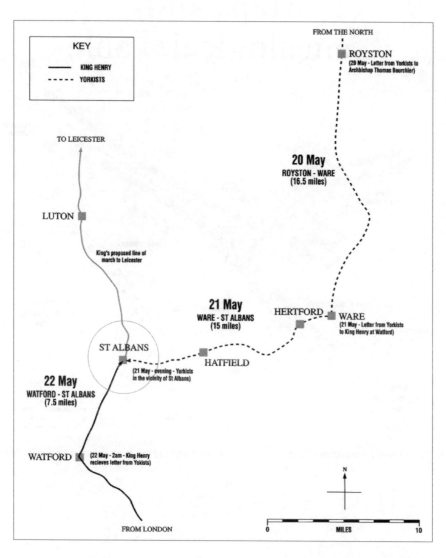

2 The first battle of St Albans, 1455. Movements of the opposing forces 20–22 May.

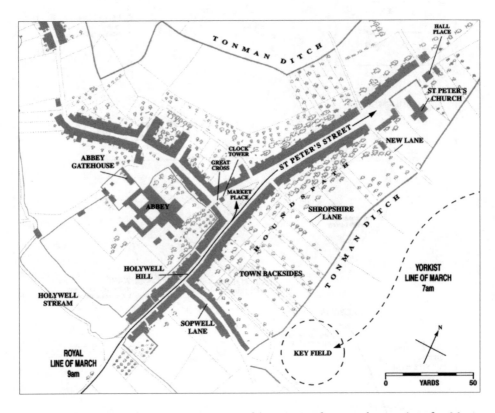

3 The first battle of St Albans, 1455. Movements of the opposing forces on the morning of 22 May.

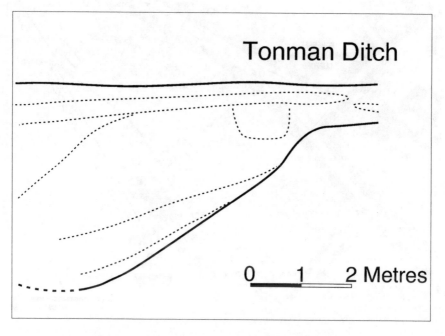

4 Diagram of the excavation dug across the Tonman Ditch.

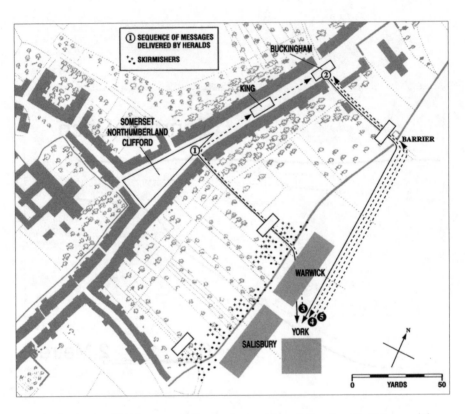

5 The first battle of St Albans, 1455. The opening positions during the negotiations and the preliminary skirmishing.

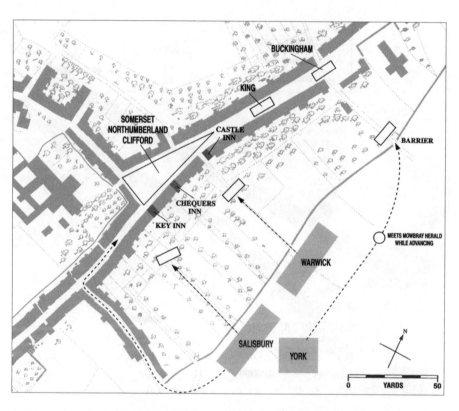

6 The first battle of St Albans, 1455. Movements of the Yorkist forces.

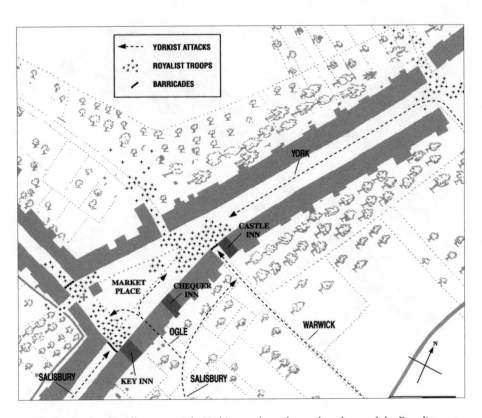

7 The first battle of St Albans, 1455. The Yorkist attack on the market place and the Royalist rout.

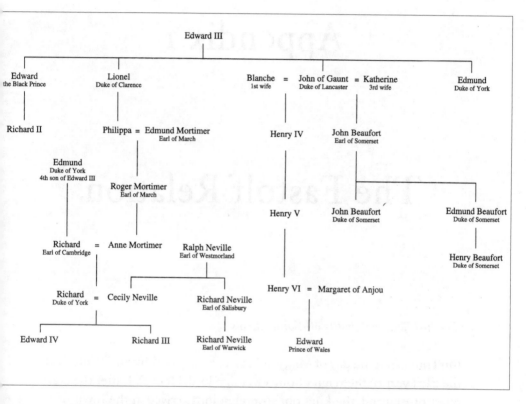

8 A simplified genealogical chart of the contending houses of York and Lancaster.

Appendix 1

The Fastolf Relation

The first 'journey' [battle of] Saint Albans

On Thursday 22nd day of May, just before the day of Whitsun [Pentecost], the 23rd year of the reign of our sovereign lord, Henry VI, after the conquest of England, the king our sovereign lord arrived at the town of St Albans by eleven [or nine] in the morning, and in his company were my lords the dukes of Buckingham and Somerset, my lords the earls of Pembroke, of Stafford, of Dorset, of Northumberland, of Devonshire and of Wiltshire, the lords of Roos, Clifford, Berners, Sudeley and Fauconberg [Falconbridge], master John Ormond, Sir Richard Harrington, controller of the King's household, Sir Bertin Entwistle, John Hanford and William Lucy, knights, and several [many?] others.

(Item) Likewise, on the same day, at more or less the same time, arrived near the town of St Albans, my lord the Duke of York, and in his company were my lords the earls of Warwick and Salisbury, and several knights and bannerets, bachelor esquires and several others. They did not enter the town of St Albans, but remained in attendance near the town, within a crossbows shot.

(Item) Likewise, as soon as the Duke of Somerset had knowledge of my lord of York's approach near the place, the aforementioned Duke of Somerset sent Lesparre pursuivant of arms to my lord Duke of Exeter, to the said Duke of York, to command him in the name and on behalf of the king, our lord, that he and all his company should quit at once and withdraw, on pain of their allegiance and breach of honour, and all being false to the king, our lord. And as soon as the said pursuivant was gone, once more came before my lord of York, Buckingham the herald, and in his company Joyeulx, pursuivant to my lord of Bonville and they delivered the same message and order, as had done pursuivant Lesparre. Thereupon, my lord of York ordered the herald and pursuivant to swear upon their duty, to say and declare to him whether this order was spoken by the king, our lord, himself, and whether they had come upon his explicit orders. And they answered that they had not and that my lord of Buckingham and my lord of Somerset had sent them to say they were coming from before the king our lord having received this order from him. To which my lord answered: 'Tell the king our lord and his cousin Buckingham that I have come here to settle my petitions and requests, and do loyal service to the king, our lord. And if I knew any in my company who would want to act to the contrary, I would punish him myself, as an example to the others.'

(Item) Likewise, my lord of York had Mowbray, herald of my lord the Duke of Norfolk, called at once and bade him go before the king our lord, to tell him that he commended himself and his noble and good grace, as humbly as any man could do, to his sovereign lord, as well as to all the lords in his company. And he was beseeching and imploring him, very humbly, that if might please his kind to grace grant him the petitions, requests and demands that he had in the past sent to him, by my lord of Fauconberge and others in his company.

(Item) Likewise, these things being said to the king our lord, by Mowbray herald, he answered that he had not seen these petitions, and bade him go to my lord of Buckingham saying that he had entrusted him for this day to give answer to all matters that should be answered in his name.

(Item) Likewise, when Mowbray came before my lord of Buckingham and said and declared his full message, my lord of Buckingham answered to him that it was true that the king our lord had not seen the petitions and requests yet and that he himself, would soon show them in diligence to the king, our lord, and would send the answer made to them back to my lord of York by Buckingham herald, saying then this to Mowbray herald, 'You will commend me to my brothers-in-law, York and Salisbury, to my nephew Warwick, and his brother Norfolk, in case he should be in their company, as you say he is nearby, that is to say that they can clearly be seen, since the king is present, and they will see his own person and banner on the field, as they withdraw to Barnet or Hatfield, for one night, waiting for some appointment to be made, or one or two men of state and honour to be sent before one to speak with them.' Thereupon the herald asked him, 'My lord, please you bid me something else for this time,' and he answered: 'Yes, I want you to commend me to my brother Norfolk and tell him that we are so next of kin that if he had a daughter and I had one, we would not marry each others daughter without a licence from the Pope, and furthermore, he married my sister. That I beseech him to have out of his heart all melancholy thoughts, wrath, and anger for this time, and the king will be grateful to him, and take him into better grace.' This being said, Mowbray herald asked him again, 'My lord, please you bid me more to say before my lords.' And he answered, 'Yes, we want everyone to know that we have come here to support no one, nor for any other cause else, but to be in the company of the king, our lord, as we are rightfully bound to, and as is meet.' Thereupon the herald took his leave and returned before my lord of York to whom he delivered his report, as afore stated.

(Item) Likewise, my lord of York immediately sent back Mowbray herald, for a second time, before my lord of Buckingham, begging him to be willing to go before the king our lord, in order to get an answer to his requests and petitions. Thereupon my lord of Buckingham answered to the herald that he would with all possible dispatch send his answer by his herald Buckingham, to my lord of York, which he never did.

(Item) Likewise, because the answer was not sent along, the company of my lord of York was made uneasy, saying, that it was only a delay. It is the reason why my lord of York sent back Mowbray for a third time, before my lord of Buckingham, asking him to answer his petitions, with no more delay. And when Mowbray herald came to the gate [*barriere*:

barrier, bar] of the town of St Albans, which is near the town parish church, he found there, Sir Richard Harrington, Bertin Entwistle and John Hanford knights, Breknok squire and John Swythman who asked the herald what he wanted. And he answered that he wanted to speak to my lord of Buckingham. And they said to him that he would instantly speak with him, and they sent him before my lord of Buckingham, who immediately ordered the master of his household and a knight called Sir Thomas Fynderne to go before Mowbray herald.

On his arrival Mowbray told him the reason why he had come. Thereupon they returned to my lord of Buckingham and kept the herald waiting till they came back. After going to my lord of Buckingham, they returned before the herald and told him that my lord of Buckingham had been before the king our lord, who was not decided to give them any answer. Thereupon the herald took his leave. As he returned he found my lord of York and all his company coming towards the town of St Albans and the herald gave the answer to my lord of York. Thereupon he replied, 'Therefore we must do what we can do.' Thereupon they made their way towards the town etc.

Fastolf Relation, College of Arms, *Arundel MS* 48, folio 342. (Translated from the French by Michele Seeberger).

Appendix 2

The Dijon Relation

When the Duke of Somerset and those who were of his party then being in the City of London, heard that the Duke of York and many other lords in his company were advancing against them with a force of five thousand men, and when he considered what he had done against the Duke of York and that he was also in very bad odour with the people of London, he came to the conclusion that he should not remain in the City of London for fear that the people would fall on him the moment he [York] arrived. For which cause he persuaded the king to sally forth against the said Duke of York and his other enemies, their opponents, and hastily gathered the said third day after the feast of the Ascension up to 3,500 persons and on the 21st day of May in the morning they issued out of London and went to lodge twenty miles away from there at a little village where there is an abbey called St Albans, near the which village at less than half a day's march their enemies were lodged. These, when they knew of the king's coming, immediately approached him and also the 22nd day of the said month very early the king sent a herald to the Duke of York to know the cause for which he had come there with so many men and that it seemed to the king something quite new that he, the duke, should be rising against him, the king. The reply made was that he was not coming against him thus, [he] was always ready to do him obedience but he well intended in one way or another to have the traitors who were about him so that they should be punished, and that in case he could not have them with good will and fair consent, he intended in any case to have them by force. The reply that was made from the king's side to the said Duke of York was that he [the king] was unaware that there were any traitors about him were it not for the Duke of York himself who had risen against the crown. And even before this reply came to the Duke of York there began a skirmish before the village by one side and the other. And thus when the Duke of York had the aforesaid reply the battle became more violent and both sides with banners displayed began to fight. And first the Duke of York's men incontinently approached the village and set a good guard at all the ways about and entered in with such great force that incontinent they took and blockaded the marketplace of the said village and part of his people found themselves in the middle of it and in this manner began to fight the one party against the other. The battle began on the stroke of ten hours in the morning but because the place was small few of the combatants could set to work there and matters reach such a great extremity that four of those who were of the king's bodyguard were killed by arrows in his presence and the king himself was struck by an arrow in the shoulder, but it penetrated only a little of the flesh. At last when they had fought for the space of three hours the king's party seeing themselves to have the worst of it broke on one wing and began to flee and the Duke of Somerset retreated within an inn to save himself and hid. Which things seen by those of the said Duke of York [they] incontinent beset the said house all about. And there the Duke of York gave orders that the king should be taken and drawn out of the throng and put in the abbey in safety and thus it was done. And in this abbey took refuge also with him the Duke of Buckingham who was very badly wounded by three arrows. And incontinent this done [they] began to fight Somerset and his men who were in this place

within the inn and defended themselves valiantly. And in the end after
the doors were broken down the Duke of Somerset seeing that he
had no other remedy took council with his men about coming out
and did so, as a result of which incontinent he and all his people were
surrounded by the Duke of York's men. And after some were stricken
down and the Duke of Somerset had killed four of them with his own
hand, it is said, he was felled to the ground with an axe and incontinent being so wounded in several places that there he ended his life.
And while the Duke of Somerset made this defence in the inn others
of his party who remained outside all the time fought against those
of the Duke of York so that three lords died there on Somerset's side,
that is to say the Earl of Northumberland, Lord Clifford, which was a
great pity for he was a brave man, and Sir Richard Harrington also a
noble knight and a brave man and many other gentlemen and esquires
as many of one party as the other so that in all there died 200 persons
or thereabouts. The battle lasted until two and a half hours after noon
and this done the Duke of York's men took themselves to the abbey to
kill the Duke of Buckingham and the treasurer, who is called the Earl
of Wiltshire, who had retreated there with the king but the said Duke
of York would not suffer it but sent his herald to the king to inform
him that he must choose which he preferred, either to hand over the
two lords as prisoners into his hands, or that they should be killed in
front of him and to put himself in danger once more. Wherefore the
king agreed freely to allow him to arrest the said two lords and so he
did, in particular the Duke of Buckingham. The treasurer could not be
found for disguising himself he fled in a monk's habit and even now
the 27th May no one knows where he has gone. And when all these
things were done the Duke of York entered within the abbey and went
before the king's person and there went on his knees to him crying
mercy for whatever way he might have offended and for the peril in
which he had put his person and many other good and humble words,
showing him that he had not gone against him but against the traitors
to his crown, and in the end before the Duke of York went away from
there the king pardoned him everything and took him in his good
grace, and this day the king, the Duke of York and all the other lords
came to London where they have been received with great joy and
solemn procession. And the said Duke of York will now be without
contradiction the first after the king and will have the government of

all. God give him grace to carry out his tasks well and have pity on the souls of sinners. Amen.

The Dijon Relation, *Archives de la Cote d'Or*, Dijon, B.11942, no.258 (French).

Appendix 3

Whethamstede's *Registrum*

After an invented speech given by the duke of York to his allies, the earls of Warwick and Salisbury, in which the duke of Somerset is attacked, Abbot John Whethamstede continues:

This speech was pleasing to the ears of the Earls [and] rising up, they came with him to meet the King at the town of St Albans; and there, uniting themselves and their men into one [force] to the number of almost 3,000 fighting men in a field which faces the middle of the town towards the East they held a council among themselves [to discuss] how they could rush into the town and there take the prey they were after.

Meanwhile, while they had halted for their discussion, the King, informed of their arrival, sent the Duke of Buckingham to them, and he asked them whether their arrival was peaceful, or arising from some other opposite intention. They all answered the same thing, saying, 'We are faithful liege men of the King, we intend him no evil, nor have we come here for this reason, to do him any harm. Only let there be given to us that wicked man who has lost Normandy, who has neglected Gascony, and who has led and misled this kingdom of England to this wretched state... Let that man be given to us, and we shall return again peacefully to our own without the turmoil of a struggle, or the damaging of peace. But if not, if a refusal be given to us in this our desire, and the King is unwilling for any reasons now stated to lose him, then he is to know that we would prefer rather to go into the field than to return to our own, our proposal frustrated, without our desired prey'.

The King, informed of their words and desires, and understanding these to be their will rather than reasonable or lawful, chose rather to make trial of the doubtful outcome of battle [i.e. risk a battle] than to agree [be willing] either to lose the said Duke, or hand him over into the hands of his enemies. Realizing this, they soon sounded the trumpet and rushed into the middle of St Peter's Street, breaking down the barriers [*abruptis obstaculis*] until they had the King's battle-line in front of them. They fought each other for a short space of time so fiercely that here you would have seen one man lying with his brain struck out, there another with his arm cut off, there a third with his throat cut, there a fourth with his chest pierced, and the whole place [square] beyond filled with corpses of the slain, on this side and that and everywhere in every direction. And so powerfully at the time was shield driven back by shield and targe by targe, threatening sword by sword, foot by foot and weapon-point by weapon-point that for a tiny little pause of time the outcome was in doubt to which side victory would yield, and the dice of fate was unclear enough.

At last, however, by some terror sent from heaven, or breath of madness implanted or innate, turning their backs they [the king's men] fled in great numbers – nay, the greater part, on the king's side, running about through the gardens and fields, the brambles and thickets, the hedges and woods, sought for themselves places and hideouts where they could best lurk and conceal themselves until the storm of the whole battling had stopped. Among whom there were some of knightly rank, men of elegant enough appearance in themselves, but more like Paris than Hector in nature. To whom because,

'It had been more [gentle] to have lain on a soft bed
And to have held a tender girl in folded arms
Than to have loaded their right shoulders with shields or spears
Or to have supported a helmet on their flattened hair'

So pursuing softness rather than service, and more often frequenting the park [i.e. hunting] than the combat of the next battle...they abandoned the king in the field, and even sought out-of-the-way places to hide in for themselves. There were even also others from the king's household, or palace, who all, as in a greater [matter] because they were clothed for gentle activities, thus from the softness of their spirit shuddering away from the sight of blood, took themselves off from the field lest they should see its spilling. There were moreover even a third group, from the eastern region of the kingdom who, because for the reason of their origin were softer than the rest, and more tender, according to that saying of the poet,

Whatever faces the Eastern regions, and the warmth of the kingdom
The mildness of the sky softens their spirits.

So, struck by the spirit of fear, they left their superior lord alone on the field; and they fled from him in the same way as sheep or little lambs are accustomed to flee from the shepherd, when they have seen a wolf coming.

The king, however, seeing his men, just about all, either turned in flight or dead on the field, and that he was standing under his standard without any protection, without hope or relief, on the suggestion of a few who had remained that he should flee from the face of the bow, and escape from the dangers of the arrows, which kept flying about his head more thickly than snowflakes, took himself off to the tiny dwelling of a tanner and there stayed with his men, until the Duke of York came and greeted him in these words, and comforted him...

John Whethamstede, *Registrum Abbatiae Johannis Whethamstede Secundae*, ed. H.T. Riley, Vol. 1, 1872–3. (Translated from the Latin by Lesley Boatwright).

Notes

Chapter 1: York and Somerset

1   H. Ellis, ed., *Original Letters Illustrative of English History*, First
        Series, I, 1827, pp. 11–13.

2   *Ibid.*

3   Dominic Mancini, *The Usurpation of Richard the Third*, ed. C.A.J.
        Armstrong, second edition, 1969, p. 95.

4   The text of Blacman's work is printed in *Duo Rerum
        Anglicarum Scriptores Veteres*, ed. T. Hearne, Vol. 1, 1732, pp. 285–
        307. See also *Henry the Sixth, a reprint of John Blacman's Memoir*,
        with translation and notes by M.R. James, 1919.

5   H. Ellis, ed., *The Chronicle of John Hardyng*, 1812, p. 410.

6   C.L. Kingsford, 'Extracts from the first version of Hardyng's
        Chronicle', *English Historical Review*, 27, 1912, pp. 744–5.

7   J. Gairdner, ed., *The Paston Letters*, Vol. 2, 1904, p. 147.

8   J. Gairdner, ed., *Three Fifteenth Century Chronicles*, 1880, p. 94.

9   H. Ellis, ed., *Original Letters Illustrative of English History*, First
        Series, I, 1827, pp. 11–13.

10   *Ibid.*

11   C.L. Kingsford, 'London Chronicle for 1446–1452', *English Historical literature in the Fifteenth Century*, 1913, pp.297-8.

12   J. Stevenson, ed., 'Annales Rerum Anglicarum' ('The Wars of the English in France'), *Rolls Series*, Vol. 2, 1864, p.770.

Chapter 2: The Beginning of Sorrows

1   J.C. Atkinson, ed., *Cartularium Abbathiae de Whitby*, II, 1879, pp.694-695.

2   G.M. Trevelyan, *History of England*, 1945, p.259.

3   R.A. Griffiths, 'Local Rivalries and National Politics: The Percies, the Nevilles and The Duke of Exeter', *Speculum*, Vol. XLIII, 4, 1968, p.589.

4   R. Flenley, ed., 'Bale's Chronicle' in *Six Town Chronicles of England*, 1911, p.141.

5   J. Gairdner, ed., *The Paston Letters*, Vol. 2, 1904, p.297.

6   J. Strachey, ed., *Rotuli Parliamentorum*, Vol. 5, 1783, p.280.

7   The Dijon Relation, Archives de la Cote d'Or, Dijon, B.11942, no.258 (French). Cited by C.A.J. Armstrong in 'Politics and the Battle of St Albans, 1455', *Bulletin of the Institute of Historical Research*, Vol. 33, no.87, 1960, p.63.

8   M.D. Harris, ed., *The Coventry Leet Book*, E.E.T.S., 1907–13, p.282.

9   *Ibid.*

10   J. Strachey, ed., *Rotuli Parliamentorum*, Vol. 5, 1783, pp.280-81.

Chapter 3: Faith, Allegiance and Duty

1   J. Gairdner, ed., 'Stow Relation', *The Paston Letters*, Vol. 3, 1904, p.25.

2   J. Strachey, ed., *Rotuli Parliamentorum*, Vol. 5, 1783, p.280.

3   *Ibid.*, p.281.

4   J.S. Davies, ed., *An English Chronicle of the Reigns of Richard II, Henry IV, Henry V, and Henry VI*, 1856, p.71.

5   A.B. Hinds, ed., *Calendar of State Papers and Manuscripts existing in the Archives and Collections of Milan*, Vol. 1, 1912, p.16-17.

6   J. Gairdner, ed., Phillipps Relation, *The Paston Letters*, Vol. 3, 1904, p.30.

7   A.C. Reeves, ed., 'Some of Humphrey Stafford's Military
     Indentures', *Nottingham Medieval Studies*, Vol. 16, 1972, p.91.

8   H.M. Cam, 'The Decline and Fall of English Feudalism',
     History, 25, 1940, p.225.

9   J. Gairdner, ed., Phillipps Relation, *The Paston Letters*, Vol 3,
     1904, p.30.

10   R.L. Storey, *The End of the House of Lancaster*, 1986, p.122.

11   J. Gairdner, ed., Phillipps Relation, *The Paston Letters*, Vol 3,
     1904, p.30.

Chapter 4: St Albans

1   C. Oman, *The Political History of England, 1377–1485*, 1920,
     p.367.

2   H.T. Riley, ed., *Gesta Abbatum Monasterii Sancti Albani*, Rolls
     Series, Vol. 3, 1867–8, p.355-6.

3   *Ibid.*

4   W. Page, 'The Marian survey of St Albans', *Trans. St Albans and
     Herts. Architectural and Archaeological Society.*, 1893–1902, pp.8-24.

5   J. Gairdner, ed., Stow Relation, *The Paston Letters*, Vol. 3, 1904,
     p.25.

6   Fastolf Relation, College of Arms, *Arundel MS.* 48, folio 341.

7   See Stow Relation, Chancery Miscellanea, PRO, C47/37/3/4-
     11; also M.L. Kekewich, C. Richmond, A.F. Sutton, L.
     Visser-Fuchs, J.L. Watts, *'John Vales Book'*, *The Politics of
     Fifteenth-Century England*, 1995.

8   J. Gairdner, ed., Stow Relation, *The Paston Letters*, Vol. 3, 1904,
     p.25.

9   J. Strachey, ed., *Rotuli Parliamentorum*, Vol. 5, 1783, p.347.

10   J. Gairdner, ed., Stow Relation, *The Paston Letters*, Vol. 3, 1904,
     p.25.

11   Fastolf Relation, College of Arms, *Arundel MS.* 48, folio 341.

12   J.S. Davies, ed., *An English Chronicle of the Reigns of Richard II,
     Henry IV, Henry V, and Henry VI*, 1856, p.71

13   C.A.J. Armstrong, 'Politics and the Battle of St Albans, 1455',
     Bulletin of the Institute of Historical Research, Vol. 33, no.87, 1960,
     p.25.

Chapter 5: 'I Shall Destroy Them, Every Mother's Son'

1   Fastolf Relation, College of Arms, *Arundel MS.* 48, folio 341.

2   C.A.J. Armstrong, 'Politics and the Battle of St Albans, 1455',
     Bulletin of the Institute of Historical Research, Vol. 33, no.87, 1960.

3   M.A. Hicks, 'Propaganda and the First Battle of St Albans',
     Nottingham Medieval Studies, Vol. 44, 2000.

4   C.A.J. Armstrong, 'Politics and the Battle of St Albans, 1455',
     Bulletin of the Institute of Historical Research, Vol. 33, no.87, 1960,
     p.1.

5   J. Gairdner, ed., Phillipps Relation, *The Paston Letters*, Vol. 3,
     1904, p.29.

6   *Ibid.*

7   Fastolf Relation, College of Arms, *Arundel MS.* 48, folio 342.

8   A.H. Thomas and I.D. Thornley, eds, *The Great Chronicle of
     London*, 1983, p.187.

9   J. Gairdner, ed., Stow Relation, *The Paston Letters*, Vol. 3, 1904,
     p.25.

10   *Ibid.*, p.29.

11   J.S. Davies, ed., *An English Chronicle of the Reigns of Richard II,
     Henry IV, Henry V, and Henry VI*, 1856, p.71.

12   Fastolf Relation, College of Arms, *Arundel MS.* 48, folio 341.

13   Namely the Dijon Relation, Thomas Gascoigne, John
     Whethamstede and *Davies' Chronicle*.

14   Fastolf Relation, College of Arms, *Arundel MS.* 48, folio 341.

15   *Ibid.*

16   J. Gairdner, ed., Stow Relation, *The Paston Letters*, Vol. 3, 1904,
     p.26. See also Stow Relation, Chancery Miscellanea, PRO,
     C47/37/3/4-11 and M.L. Kekewich, C. Richmond, A.F.
     Sutton, L. Visser-Fuchs, J.L. Watts, *'John Vales Book', The Politics
     of Fifteenth-Century England*, 1995, 191.

17   Fastolf Relation, College of Arms, *Arundel MS.* 48, folio 341.

18   *Ibid.*

19   J. Gairdner, ed., Stow Relation, *The Paston Letters*, Vol. 3, 1904,
     pp.26-27. See also Stow Relation, Chancery Miscellanea,
     PRO, C47/37/3/4-11, and M.L. Kekewich, C. Richmond, A.F.
     Sutton, L. Visser-Fuchs, J.L. Watts, *'John Vales Book', The Politics
     of Fifteenth-Century England*, 1995, 191.

20   Fastolf Relation, College of Arms, *Arundel MS.* 48, folio 342.
21   *Ibid.*

Chapter 6: 'A Warwick, A Warwick'

1   The Dijon Relation, Archives de la Cote d'Or, Dijon, B. 11942,
      no.258 (French). Cited by C.A.J. Armstrong in 'Politics and
      the Battle of St Albans, 1455', *Bulletin of the Institute of Historical
      Research*, Vol. 33, no.87, 1960, p.63.
2   J. Gairdner, ed., Stow Relation, *The Paston Letters*, Vol. 3, 1904,
      p.25.
3   Fastolf Relation, College of Arms, *Arundel MS.* 48, folio 342.
4   The Dijon Relation, Archives de la Cote d'Or, Dijon, B. 11942,
      no.258 (French). Cited by C.A.J. Armstrong in 'Politics and
      the Battle of St Albans, 1455', *Bulletin of the Institute of Historical
      Research,* Vol. 33, no.87, 1960, p.63.
5   A.H. Thomas and I.D. Thornley, eds, *The Great Chronicle of
      London*, 1983, p.187.
6   J. Gairdner, ed., Stow Relation, *The Paston Letters*, Vol. 3, 1904,
      p.27.
7   J. Gairdner, ed., 'Gregory's Chronicle', *The Historical Collections
      of a Citizen of London*, 1876, p.198.
8   J. Gairdner, ed., Stow Relation, *The Paston Letters*, Vol. 3, 1904,
      p.28.
9   J. Gairdner, ed., Phillipps Relation, *The Paston Letters*, Vol. 3,
      1904, p.30.
10   Fastolf Relation, College of Arms, *Arundel MS.* 48, folio 342.
11   J. Gairdner, ed., Stow Relation, *The Paston Letters*, Vol. 3, 1904,
      pp.27–28.
12   A.H. Thomas and I.D. Thornley, eds, *The Great Chronicle of
      London*, 1983, p.187.
13   J. Gairdner, ed., Stow Relation, *The Paston Letters*, Vol. 3, 1904,
      p.28.
14   J. Gairdner, ed., Phillipps Relation, *The Paston Letters*, Vol. 3,
      1904, p.30.
15   J.S. Davies, ed., *An English Chronicle of the Reigns of Richard II,
      Henry IV, Henry V, and Henry VI*, 1856, p.72.
16   The Dijon Relation, Archives de la Cote d'Or, Dijon, B. 11942,

no.258 (French). Cited by C.A.J. Armstrong in 'Politics and the Battle of St Albans, 1455', in *Bulletin of the Institute of Historical Research*, Vol. 33, no.87, 1960, p.64.

17   John Whethamstede, *Registrum Abbatiae Johannis Whethamstede Secundae*, ed. H.T. Riley, Vol. 1, 1872–3, p.168.

18   J.S. Davies, ed., *An English Chronicle of the Reigns of Richard II, Henry IV, Henry V, and Henry VI*, 1856, p.72.

19   The Dijon Relation, Archives de la Cote d'Or, Dijon, B.11942, no.258 (French). Cited by C.A.J. Armstrong in 'Politics and the Battle of St Albans, 1455', *Bulletin of the Institute of Historical Research*, Vol. 33, no.87, 1960, p.64.

20   J. Gairdner, ed., *Gregory's Chronicle, The Historical Collections of a Citizen of London*, 1876, p.198.

21   The Dijon Relation, Archives de la Cote d'Or, Dijon, B.11942, no.258 (French). Cited by C.A.J. Armstrong in 'Politics and the Battle of St Albans, 1455', in *Bulletin of the Institute of Historical Research*, Vol. 33, no.87, 1960, p.64.

22   John Whethamstede, *Registrum Abbatiae Johannis Whethamstede Secundae*, ed. H.T. Riley, Vol. 1, 1872–3, p.169.

23   The Dijon Relation, Archives de la Cote d'Or, Dijon, B.11942, no.258 (French). Cited by C.A.J. Armstrong in 'Politics and the Battle of St Albans, 1455', in *Bulletin of the Institute of Historical Research*, Vol. 33, no.87, 1960, p.64.

24   J.S. Davies, ed., *An English Chronicle of the Reigns of Richard II, Henry IV, Henry V, and Henry VI*, 1856, p.72.

25   A.B. Hinds, ed., *Calendar of State Papers and Manuscripts existing in the Archives and Collections of Milan*, Vol. 1, 1912, p.17.

26   J. Gairdner, ed., *Gregory's Chronicle, The Historical Collections of a Citizen of London*, 1876, pp.198-99.

27   H. Ellis, ed., *The Chronicle of John Hardyng*, 1812, p.402.

28   The Dijon Relation, Archives de la Cote d'Or, Dijon, B.11942, no.258 (French). Cited by C.A.J. Armstrong in 'Politics and the Battle of St Albans, 1455', *Bulletin of the Institute of Historical Research*, Vol. 33, no.87, 1960, p.64.

29   J. Gairdner, ed., Stow Relation, *The Paston Letters*, Vol 3, 1904, p.28.

30   The Dijon Relation, Archives de la Cote d'Or, Dijon, B.11942, no.258 (French). Cited by C.A.J. Armstrong in 'Politics and

the Battle of St Albans, 1455', *Bulletin of the Institute of Historical Research*, Vol. 33, no.87, 1960, p.64.

31   J. Gairdner, ed., Stow Relation, *The Paston Letters*, Vol 3, 1904, p.29.

Chapter 7: The Fate of the Kingdom

1   W. Stubbs, *The Constitutional History of England*, Vol. 3, 1903, p.176.

2   J. Gairdner, ed., Phillipps Relation, *The Paston Letters*, Vol. 3, 1904, p.30.

3   N.H. Nicolas, E. Tyrell, eds, *Chronicle of London 1089–1483*, 1827, p.139.

4   J. Gairdner, ed., Stow Relation, *The Paston Letters*, Vol. 3, 1904, p.28.

5   The Dijon Relation, Archives de la Cote d'Or, Dijon, B.11942, no.258 (French). Cited by C.A.J. Armstrong in 'Politics and the Battle of St Albans, 1455', *Bulletin of the Institute of Historical Research*, Vol. 33, no.87, 1960, p.64.

6   J.S. Davies, ed., *An English Chronicle of the Reigns of Richard II, Henry IV, Henry V, and Henry VI*, 1856, p.72.

7   J. Gairdner, ed., *The Paston Letters*, Vol 3, 1904, p.31.

8   W.E. Hampton, *Memorials of the Wars of the Roses*, 1979, p.87.

9   F. Yeoman, 'Skeletons in Armour', *The Ricardian, Journal of the Richard III Society*, no. 28, 1970, p.8.

10   J. Gairdner, ed., Phillipps Relation, *The Paston Letters*, Vol. 3, 1904, p.30.

11   J. Gairdner, ed., *Gregory's Chronicle, The Historical Collections of a Citizen of London*, 1876, p.198.

12   A.B. Hinds, ed., *Calendar of State Papers and Manuscripts existing in the Archives and Collections of Milan*, Vol. 1, 1912, p.17.

13   J. Gairdner, ed., *The Paston Letters*, Vol. 3, 1904, p.32.

14   Jean-Philippe Genet, 'New Politics or New Language? The words of politics in Yorkist and early Tudor England', in *The End of the Middle Ages? England in the Fifteenth and Sixteenth Centuries*, ed. J.L. Watts, 1998, p.52.

15   J. Strachey, ed., *Rotuli Parliamentorum*, Vol. 5, 1783, p.282.

16   *Ibid.*, p.280.

17   J. Gairdner, ed., *The Paston Letters*, Vol. 3, 1904, p.44.
18   T. Rymer, ed., *Foedera*, Vol. 5, 2, 1704–13, p.64.
19   J. Strachey, ed., *Rotuli Parliamentorum*, Vol. 5, 1783, p.347.
20   W. Shakespeare, *Richard III*, Act 1, Scene 1.

Bibliography

Primary Sources

C.A.J. Armstrong, ed., Dominic Mancini, *The Usurpation of Richard the Third*, second edition, 1969.

J.C. Atkinson, ed., *Cartularium Abbathiae de Whitby*, II, 1879.

W. Brigg, 'Register of the Archdeacons of St Albans', *The Herts Genealogist and Antiquary*, i, 1895.

J.S. Davies, ed., *An English Chronicle of the Reigns of Richard II, Henry IV, Henry V, and Henry VI*, 1856.

The Dijon Relation, *Archives de la Cote d'Or*, Dijon, B.11942, no.258 (French). Cited by C.A.J. Armstrong in 'Politics and the Battle of St Albans, 1455', *Bulletin of the Institute of Historical Research*, Vol. 33, no.87, 1960.

H. Ellis, ed., *Original Letters Illustrative of English History*, First Series, I, 1827.

—, *The Chronicle of John Hardyng*, 1812.

Fastolf Relation, College of Arms, *Arundel MS*. 48, folio 342.

R. Flenley, ed., *Bale's Chronicle*, in *Six Town Chronicles of England*, 1911.

E.B. de Fonblanque, *Annals of the House of Percy*, 1887.

J. Gairdner, ed., *Gregory's Chronicle, The Historical Collections of a Citizen of London*, 1876.

—, Phillipps Relation, *The Paston Letters*, Vol. 3, 1904.

—, Stow Relation and Phillipps Relation in *The Paston Letters*, Vol. 3, 1904.

—, *Three Fifteenth Century Chronicles*, 1880.

M.D. Harris, ed., *The Coventry Leet Book*, E.E.T.S., 1907–13.

T. Hearne, ed., *Duo Rerum Anglicarum Scriptores Veteres*, Vol. 1, 1732.

A.B. Hinds, ed., *Calendar of State Papers and Manuscripts existing in the Archives and Collections of Milan*, Vol. 1, 1912.

C.L. Kingsford, 'Extracts from the first version of Hardyng's Chronicle', in *English Historical Review*, 27, 1912.

—, 'London Chronicle for 1446–1452', *English Historical Literature in the Fifteenth Century*, 1913.

—, ed., *The Stoner Letters*, Camden Society, 3rd Series, xxix, 1919.

N.H. Nicolas, E. Tyrell, eds, *Chronicle of London 1089–1483*, 1827.

W. Pronger, 'Thomas Gascoigne', *English Historical Review*, liii, 1938.

H.T. Riley, ed., *Gesta Abbatum Monasterii Sancti Albani, Rolls Series*, Vol. 3, 1867–8.

—, John Whethamstede, *Registrum Abbatiae Johannis Whethamstede Secundae*, Vol. 1, 1872 –3.

J.E.T. Rogers, ed., Thomas Gascoigne, *Loci e Libro Veritatum*, 1881.

T. Rymer, ed., *Foedera*, Vol. 5, 2, 1704–13.

L.T. Smith, ed., *The Itinerary of John Leland 1535–1543*, 1910.

J. Strachey, ed., *Rotuli Parliamentorum*, Vol. 5, 1783.

A.H. Thomas and I.D. Thornley, eds, *The Great Chronicle of London*, 1983.

J. Weever, *Ancient Funeral Monuments*, 1767.

Secondary Sources

C.T. Allmand, ed., *War, Literature and Politics in the Late Middle Ages*, 1976.

C.A.J. Armstrong, 'Politics and the Battle of St Albans, 1455', *Bulletin of the Institute of Historical Research*, Vol. 33, no.87, 1960.

T. Billings, *St Albans Directory*, 2003.

A.W. Boardman, *The Medieval Soldier in the Wars of the Roses*, 1998.

A.H. Burne, *The Battlefields of England* (consolidated edition), 1996.

K. Cameron, *English Place Names*, 1961.

S.B. Crimes, C.D. Ross, R.A. Griffiths, eds, *Fifteenth Century England 1399–1509*, 1995.

—, *Lancastrians, Yorkists and Henry VII*, 1964.

J. Crosland, *Sir John Fastolfe: A Medieval man of Property*, 1970.

K. Dockray, *Henry VI, Margaret of Anjou and the Wars of the Roses*, 2000.

J. Gillingham, *The Wars of the Roses, Peace and Conflict in Fifteenth-Century England*, 1981.

A. Goodman, *The Wars of the Roses*, 1981.

—, *The Wars of the Roses – The Soldier's Experience*, 2005.

A. Gransden, *Historical Writing in England*, ii, 1982.

R.A. Griffiths, *The Reign of King Henry VI*, 1981.

—, 'Local Rivalries and National Politics: The Percies, the Nevilles and the Duke of Exeter, 1452–55', *Speculum*, Vol. XLIII, No.4, October 1968.

—, 'Duke Richard of York's Intentions in 1450', *Journal of Medieval History*, Vol.1, 1976.

B. Grimshaw, *The Entwistle Family*, 1924.

W.E. Hampton, *Memorials of the Wars of the Roses*, 1979.

M.A. Hicks, *Warwick the Kingmaker*, 1998.

—, 'Propaganda and the First Battle of St Albans', *Nottingham Medieval Studies*, Vol.44, 2000.

P.A. Johnson, *Duke Richard of York, 1411–1460*, 1988.

C.E. Johnston, 'Sir William Oldhall', *English Historical Review*, 25, 1910.

M.K. Jones, 'Somerset, York and the Wars of the Roses', *English Historical Review*, Vol. 14, No 411, April 1989.

M.H. Keen, *Chivalry*, 1984.

M.L. Kekewich, C. Richmond, A.F. Sutton, L. Visser-Fuchs, J.L. Watts, *'John Vales Book', The Politics of Fifteenth-Century England*, 1995.

F.G. Kitton, 'The old inns of St Albans', *Trans. St Albans and Herts. Architectural and Archaeological Society*, new series, i (1895–1902).

J.R. Lander, *The Wars of the Roses*, 1990.

H.M. Lane, 'The male journey of St Albans', *Trans. St Albans and Herts. Architectural and Archaeological Society*, 1931.

K.B. McFarlane, *The Nobility of Later Medieval England*, 1973.

—, 'Bastard Feudalism', *Bulletin of the Institute of Historical Research*, 20, 1943–45.

P.D. McGill, *Heraldic Banners of the Wars of the Roses*, 1990.

C. Munro, ed., *Letters of Queen Margaret of Anjou*, Camden Society, LXXXVI, 1863.

A.R. Myers, ed., *English Historical Documents, 1327–1485*, 1969.

C.W.C. Oman, *The Art of War in the Middle Ages*, 1991.

—, *The Political History of England, 1377–1485*, 1920.

J. Otway-Ruthven, *The King's Secretary and the Signet Office in the Fifteenth Century*, 1939.

W. Page, 'The Marian survey of St Albans', *Trans. St Albans and Herts. Architectural and Archaeological Society*, 1893–1902.

A.J. Pollard, *North-Eastern England During the Wars of the Roses*, 1990.

—, 'Percies, Nevilles and the Wars of the Roses', *History Today*, September 1993.

—, 'The Battle of St Albans 1455', *History Today*, May 2005.

M. Prestwich, *Armies and Warfare in the Middle Ages: The English Experience*, 1996.

J.H. Ramsay, *Lancaster and York*, Vol. 1, 1892.

A.C. Reeves, 'Some of Humphrey Stafford's Military Indentures', *Nottingham Medieval Studies*, Vol. 16, 1972.

J.T. Rosenthal, 'The Estates and Finances of Richard Duke of York, 1411–1460', *Studies in Medieval and Renaissance History*, Vol. 2, 1965.

C.L. Scofield, *Life and Reign of Edward IV*, 1923.

R.L. Storey, *The End of the House of Lancaster*, 1966.

—, 'The Wardens of the Marches of England towards Scotland, 1377–1489', *English Historical Review*, No. 72, October 1957.

M. Strickland, R. Hardy, *The Great Warbow*, 2003.

W. Stubbs, *The Constitutional History of England*, Vol. 3, 1903.

C.R. Swift, *Historic St Albans*, 1940.

G.M. Trevelyan, *History of England*, 1945.

J.A. Tuck, *Border Warfare – A History of Conflict on the Anglo Scottish Border*, 1979.

J.A. Tuck, A. Goodman, *War and Border Societies in the Middle Ages*, 1992.

J.L. Watts, The *End of the Middle Ages? England in the Fifteenth and*

Sixteenth Centuries, 1998.

B. Wolffe, *Henry VI*, 1981.

C.M. Woolgar, *The Great Household in Late Medieval England*, 1999.

F. Yeoman, 'Skeletons in Armour', *The Ricardian, Journal of the Richard III Society*, No.28, 1970.

P. Young, J. Adair, *Hastings to Culloden*, 1979.

List of Illustrations

Genealogical Table and Maps

Index

References to the battle are given either under specific topics or under 'St Albans'; peers and lords are listed under their family names.

TEMPUS – REVEALING HISTORY

William II Rufus, the Red King
EMMA MASON
'A thoroughly new reappraisal of a much
maligned king. The dramatic story of his life is
told with great pace and insight'
John Gillingham
£25
0 7524 3528 0

William Wallace The True Story of Braveheart
CHRIS BROWN
'A formidable new biography... sieves through
masses of medieval records to distinguish the
man from the myth' **Magnus Magnusson**
£17.99
0 7524 3432 2

Elizabeth Wydeville
The Slandered Queen
ARLENE OKERLUND
'A penetrating, thorough and wholly
convincing vindication of this unlucky queen'
Sarah Gristwood
£18.99
0 7524 3384 9

The Battle of Hastings 1066
M.K. LAWSON
'Deeply considered and provocative' **BBC
History Magazine,** Books of the Year 2003
£25
0 7524 2689 3

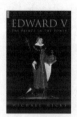

The Welsh Wars of Independence
DAIVD MOORE
'Beautifully written, subtle and remarkably
perceptive... a major re-examination of a
thousand years of Welsh history' **John Davies**
£25
0 7524 3321 0

Medieval England
From Hastings to Bosworth
EDMUND KING
'The best illustrated history of medieval
England' **John Gillingham**
£12.99
0 7524 2827 5

A Companion to Medieval England
NIGEL SAUL
'Wonderful... everything you could wish to
know about life in medieval England'
Heritage Today
£19.99
0 7524 2969 8

Edward V The Prince in the Tower
MICHAEL HICKS
'The first time in ages that a publisher has sent
me a book that I actually want to read!'
David Starkey
£25
0 7524 1996 X

If you are interested in purchasing other books published by Tempus, or in case you have difficulty finding any
Tempus books in your local bookshop, you can also place orders directly through our website:
www.tempus-publishing.com

TEMPUS – REVEALING HISTORY

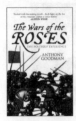   

The Wars of the Roses
The Soldiers' Experience
ANTHONY GOODMAN
'Sheds light on the lot of the common soldier as never before' *Alison Weir*

£12.99

0 7524 3731 3

The Vikings
MAGNUS MAGUNSSON
'Serious, engaging history'
BBC History Magazine

£9.99

0 7524 2699 0

William the Conqueror
DAVID BATES
'As expertly woven as the Bayeux Tapestry'
BBC History Magazine

£12.99

0 7524 2960 4

Agincourt: A New History
ANNE CURRY
'Overturns a host of assumptions about this most famous of English victories... *the* book on the battle' *Richard Holmes*

£25

0 7524 2828 4

Hereward The Last Englishman
PETER REX
'An enthralling work of historical detection'
Robert Lacey

£17.99

0 7524 3318 0

The English Resistance
The Underground War Against the Normans
PETER REX
'An invaluable rehabilitation of an ignored resistance movement' *The Sunday Times*

£12.99

0 7524 3733 X

Richard III
MICHAEL HICKS
'A most important book by the greatest living expert on Richard' *Desmond Seward*

£9.99

0 7524 2589 7

The Peasants' Revolt
England's Failed Revolution of 1381
ALASTAIR DUNN
'A stunningly good book... totally absorbing'
Melvyn Bragg

£9.99

0 7524 2965 5

If you are interested in purchasing other books published by Tempus, or in case you have difficulty finding any Tempus books in your local bookshop, you can also place orders directly through our website: www.tempus-publishing.com